One-Minute
PUZZLES

One-Minute
PUZZLES

CHARTWELL
BOOKS

This edition published in 2014 by
CHARTWELL BOOKS
an imprint of Book Sales
a division of Quarto Publishing Group USA Inc.
276 Fifth Avenue Suite 206
New York, New York 10001
USA

ISBN: 978-0-7858-3249-2
AD001775NT

Printed in China

Introduction

Life is so fast-paced that we need to make sure our brains are in good enough shape to keep up. The challenges presented in *One-Minute Puzzles* have been specially devised to accelerate your mental processes so that you are never stuck for the right answer.

We have chosen a variety of very effective puzzle types for your workout. Each of these can be solved quickly by experienced puzzlers, most of them within the target time.

But don't worry if you are off the pace to begin with – your times will improve as your brain gets used to what is demanded.

Once you get in the groove, you will lose your inhibitions and positively relish the challenge of *One-Minute Puzzles*.

Number Crunch

Starting at the top left with the number provided, work down from one box to another, applying the mathematical instructions to your running total.

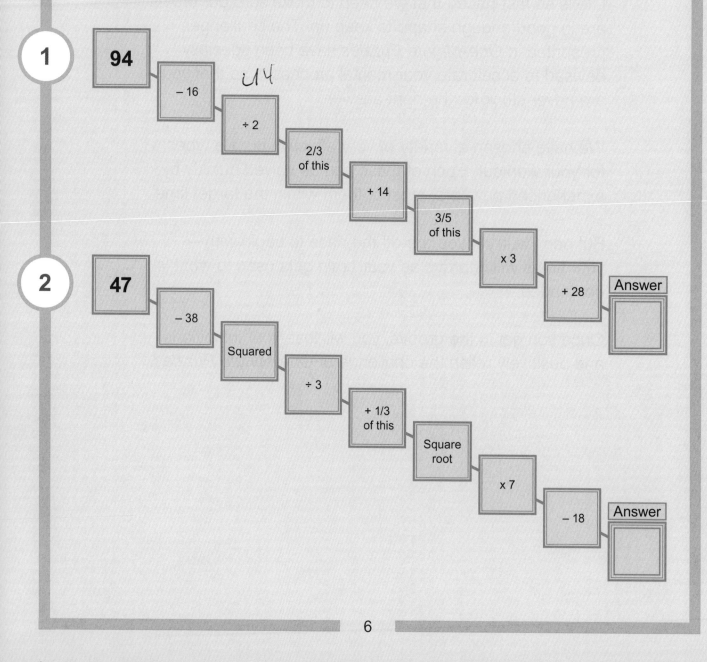

1

94

− 16

÷ 2

2/3 of this

+ 14

3/5 of this

x 3

+ 28

Answer

2

47

− 38

Squared

÷ 3

+ 1/3 of this

Square root

x 7

− 18

Answer

Pyramid Plus

The number in each circle is the sum of the two numbers below it. Just work out the missing numbers in every circle!

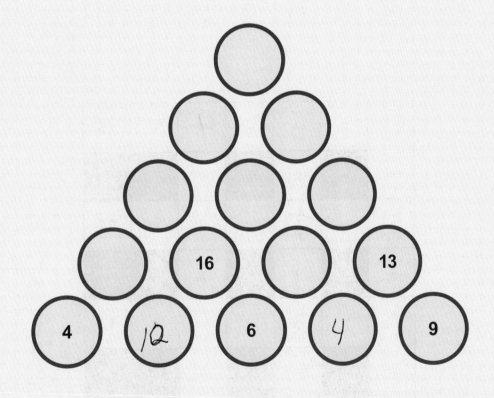

One to Nine

Using the numbers one to nine, complete these six equations (three reading across and three reading downwards). Every number is used once only, and one is already in place.

4

1 2 3 4 5 6 7 8 9

4	×	6	−	9	=	15
+		×		+		
8	−	7	×	3	=	21
−		+		×		
2	×	5	+	1	=	17
=		=		=		
10		11		84		

Summing Up

Arrange one of each of the four given numbers, as well as one each of the symbols – (minus), x (times) and + (plus) in every row and column to arrive at the answer at the end of the row or column, making the calculations in the order in which they appear. Some are already in place.

5

2 3 7 8

3	+	8	x	2	–	7	=	15
	▓		▓		▓	+	▓	▓
							=	48
	▓	+	▓		▓		▓	▓
							=	24
	▓		▓		▓		▓	▓
	2						=	12
=	▓	=	▓	=	▓	=	▓	▓
64	▓	8	▓	33	▓	27	▓	▓

9

Total Concentration

6

The blank squares below should be filled with whole numbers between 1 and 30 inclusive, any of which may occur more than once, or not at all. The numbers in every horizontal row add up to the totals on the right, as do the two long diagonal lines; whilst those in every vertical column add up to the totals along the bottom.

							119
22		1	18	23	6		121
24			27	16	24	15	138
	17	22	11	3	20		110
23	4	29			9	22	132
25	1		2	29		26	127
8	26	14	18	25		27	128
	13	19		5	19	21	100
121	103	121	104	129	116	162	133

Symbol Sums

Each symbol stands for a different number. In order to reach the correct total at the end of each row and column, what is the value of the circle, pentagon, square and star?

7

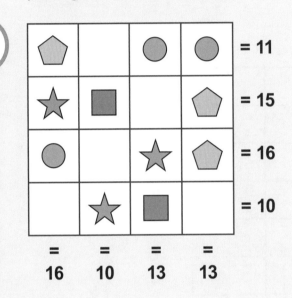

= 11
= 15
= 16
= 10

= 16 = 10 = 13 = 13

8

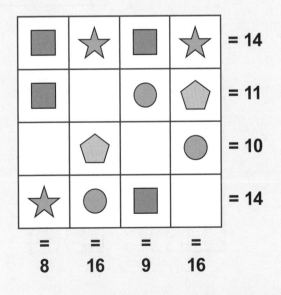

= 14
= 11
= 10
= 14

= 8 = 16 = 9 = 16

Tile Twister

Place the eight tiles into the puzzle grid so that all adjacent numbers on each tile match up. Tiles may be rotated through 360 degrees, but none may be flipped over.

9

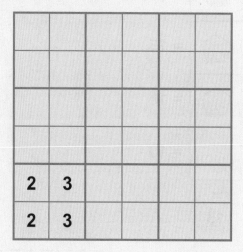

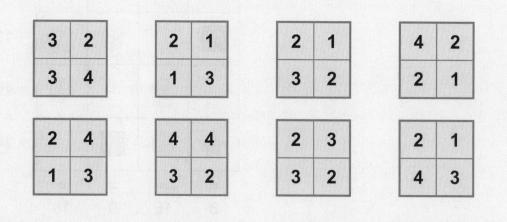

What's the Number?

In the diagram below, what number should replace the question mark?

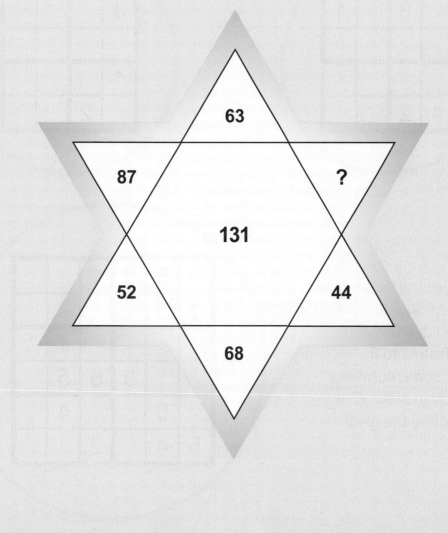

Mini Sudoku

Every row, every column and each of the four smaller boxes of four squares should be filled with a different number from 1 to 4 inclusive. Some numbers are already in place. Can you complete the grid?

11

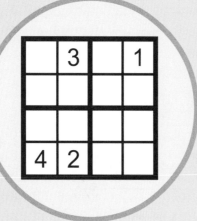

12

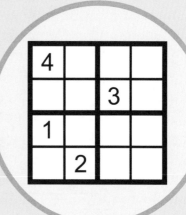

13

Every row, every column and each of the six smaller boxes of six squares should be filled with a different number from 1 to 6 inclusive. Some numbers are already in place. Can you complete the grid?

Sum Circle

Fill the three empty circles with the symbols +, – and x in some order, to make a sum which totals the number in the middle. Each symbol must be used once and calculations are made in the direction of travel (clockwise).

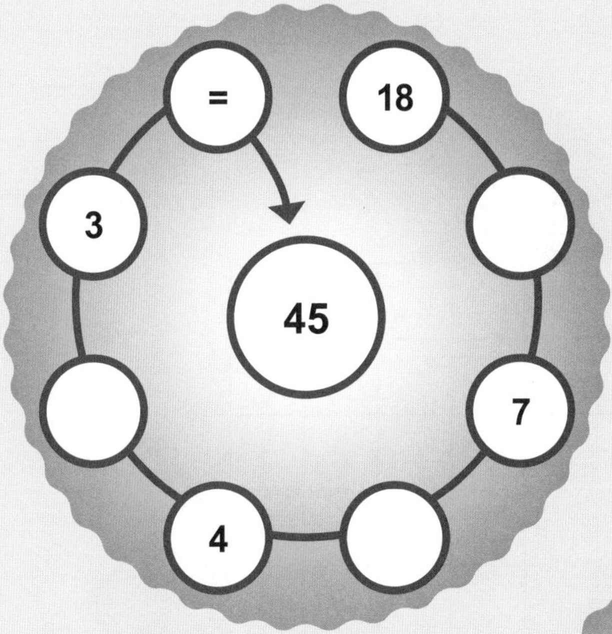

= 18

3

45

7

4

= 11

17

83

9

1

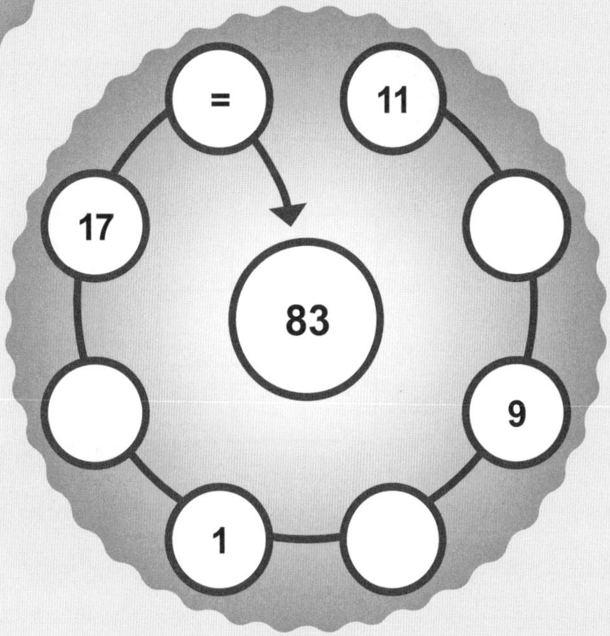

Number Path

Working from one square to another, horizontally or vertically (never diagonally), draw paths to pair up each set of two matching numbers. No path may be shared, and none may enter a square containing a number or part of another path.

16

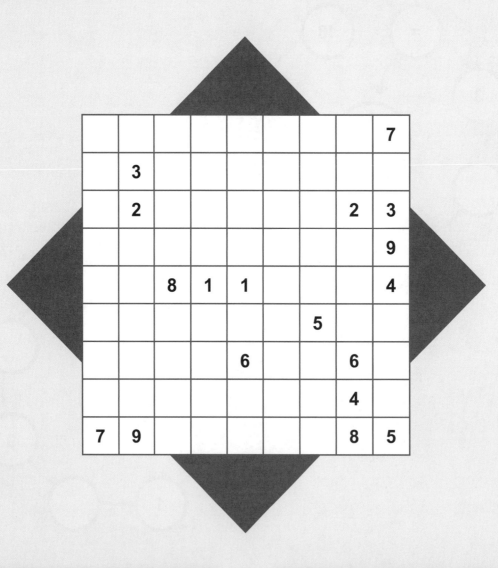

Hexagony

Can you place the hexagons into the grid, so that where any hexagon touches another along a straight line, the number in both triangles is the same? No rotation of any hexagon is allowed!

Number Crunch

Starting at the top left with the number provided, work down from one box to another, applying the mathematical instructions to your running total.

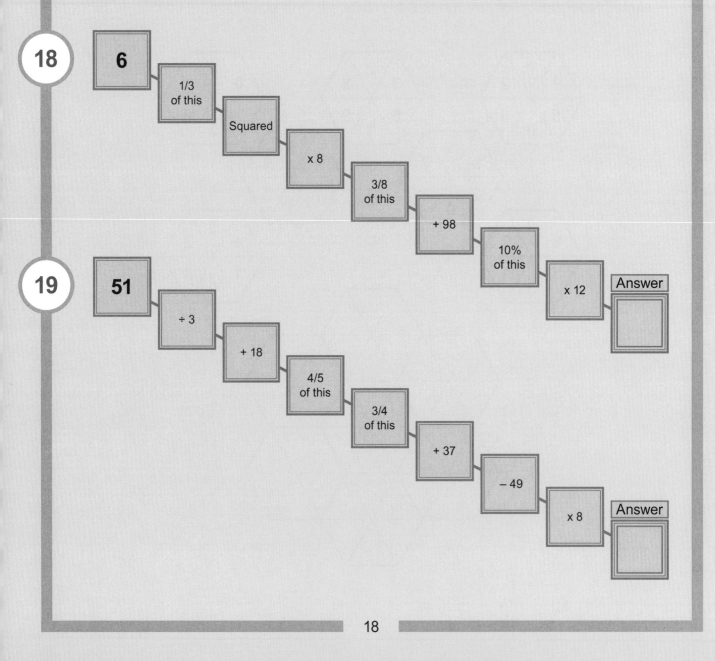

18

6 → 1/3 of this → Squared → x 8 → 3/8 of this → + 98 → 10% of this → x 12 → Answer

19

51 → ÷ 3 → + 18 → 4/5 of this → 3/4 of this → + 37 → − 49 → x 8 → Answer

Pyramid Plus

The number in each circle is the sum of the two numbers below it. Just work out the missing numbers in every circle!

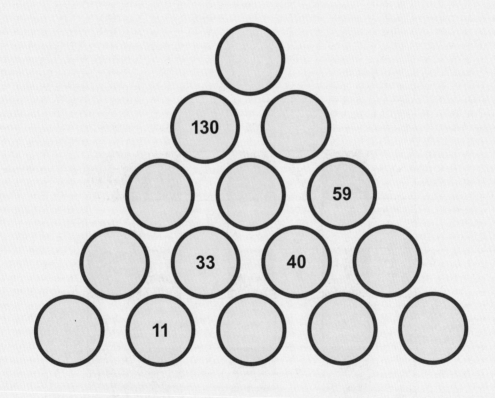

One to Nine

Using the numbers one to nine, complete these six equations (three reading across and three reading downwards). Every number is used once only, and one is already in place.

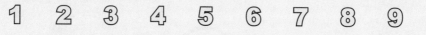

	−		x		=	35
+		+		x		
	x		+		=	21
−		x		+		
	x		−	7	=	17
=		=		=		
6		60		22		

Summing Up

Arrange one of each of the four given numbers, as well as one each of the symbols – (minus), x (times) and + (plus) in every row and column to arrive at the answer at the end of the row or column, making the calculations in the order in which they appear. Some are already in place.

3   5   6   9

5	+	9	x	3	–	6	=	36
	x			6			=	18
9							=	72
							=	32
=		=		=		=		
24		42		14		40		

Total Concentration

The blank squares below should be filled with whole numbers between 1 and 30 inclusive, any of which may occur more than once, or not at all. The numbers in every horizontal row add up to the totals on the right, as do the two long diagonal lines; whilst those in every vertical column add up to the totals along the bottom.

23

							138
18		3		2	6	22	93
2	3	17	11			11	65
12		19	10	13	5	29	111
	9	10	30	19			119
7	26		13		8		76
	14	1	5	16		8	63
27	20			9	21	28	128
82	113	83	100	66	95	116	114

Symbol Sums

Each symbol stands for a different number. In order to reach the correct total at the end of each row and column, what is the value of the circle, pentagon, square and star?

24

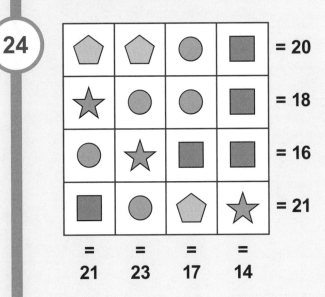

25

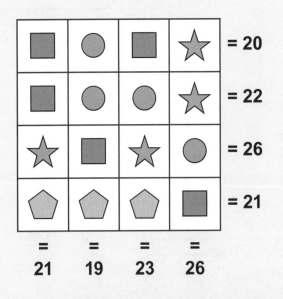

Tile Twister

Place the eight tiles into the puzzle grid so that all adjacent numbers on each tile match up. Tiles may be rotated through 360 degrees, but none may be flipped over.

26

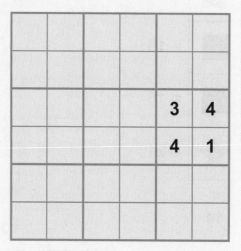

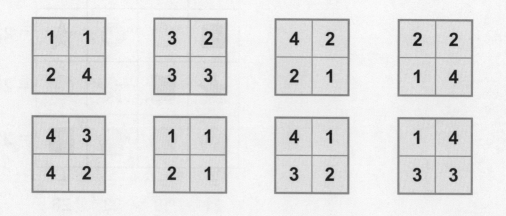

What's the Number?

In the diagram below, what number should replace the question mark?

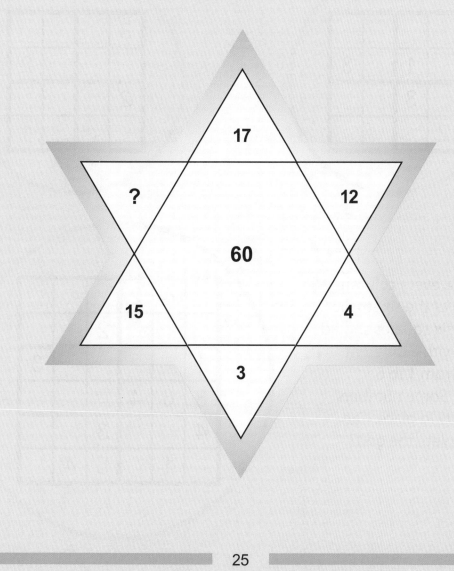

Mini Sudoku

Every row, every column and each of the four smaller boxes of four squares should be filled with a different number from 1 to 4 inclusive. Some numbers are already in place. Can you complete the grid?

28

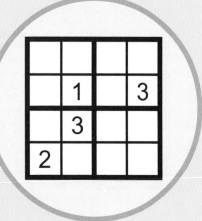

29

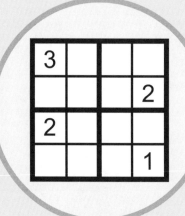

30

Every row, every column and each of the six smaller boxes of six squares should be filled with a different number from 1 to 6 inclusive. Some numbers are already in place. Can you complete the grid?

Sum Circle

Fill the three empty circles with the symbols +, – and x in some order, to make a sum which totals the number in the middle. Each symbol must be used once and calculations are made in the direction of travel (clockwise).

31

32

Circle 31: = , 16, ✱, 39, 81, 8, 2, 5, ✱

Circle 32: = , 6, +, 17, 44, 8, +, 13, +

Number Path

Working from one square to another, horizontally or vertically (never diagonally), draw paths to pair up each set of two matching numbers. No path may be shared, and none may enter a square containing a number or part of another path.

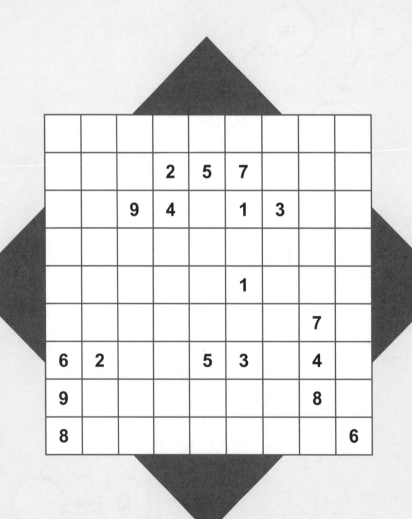

Hexagony

Can you place the hexagons into the grid, so that where any hexagon touches another along a straight line, the number in both triangles is the same? No rotation of any hexagon is allowed!

Number Crunch

Starting at the top left with the number provided, work down from one box to another, applying the mathematical instructions to your running total.

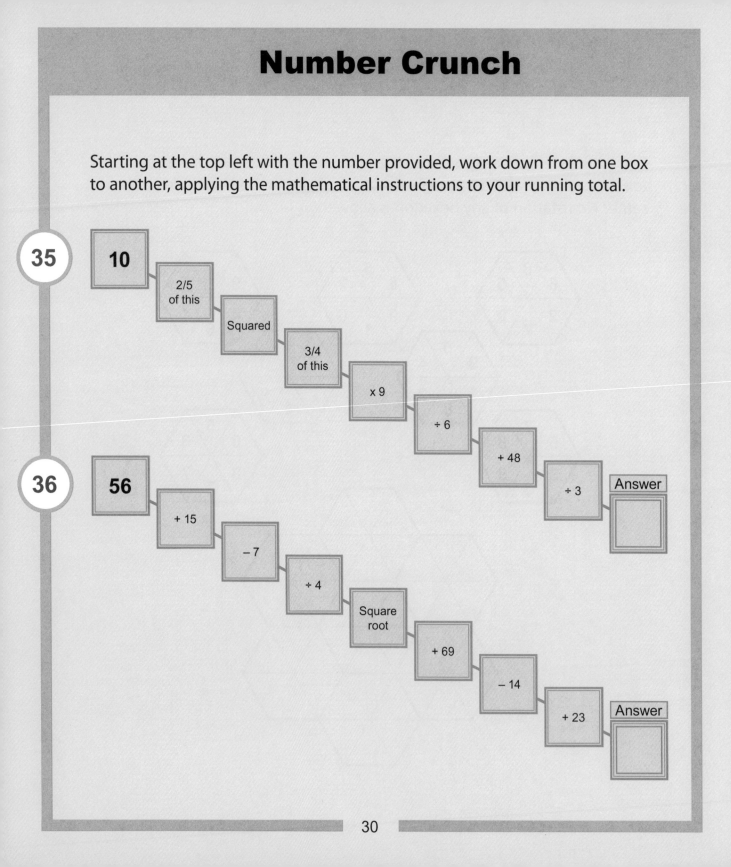

35

| 10 |
| 2/5 of this |
| Squared |
| 3/4 of this |
| x 9 |
| ÷ 6 |
| + 48 |
| ÷ 3 |
| Answer |

36

| 56 |
| + 15 |
| − 7 |
| ÷ 4 |
| Square root |
| + 69 |
| − 14 |
| + 23 |
| Answer |

Pyramid Plus

The number in each circle is the sum of the two numbers below it. Just work out the missing numbers in every circle!

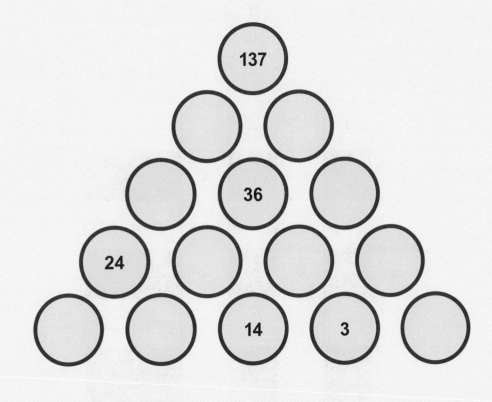

One to Nine

Using the numbers one to nine, complete these six equations (three reading across and three reading downwards). Every number is used once only, and one is already in place.

38

1 2 3 4 5 6 7 8 9

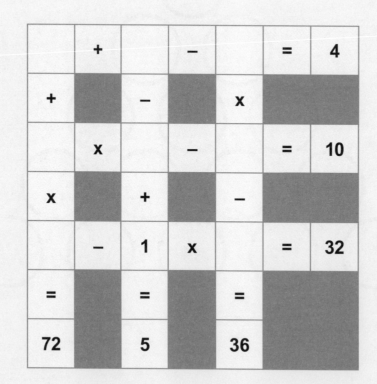

	+		−		=	4
+		−		x		
	x		−		=	10
x		+		−		
	−	1	x		=	32
=		=		=		
72		5		36		

Summing Up

Arrange one of each of the four given numbers, as well as one each of the symbols – (minus), x (times) and + (plus) in every row and column to arrive at the answer at the end of the row or column, making the calculations in the order in which they appear. Some are already in place.

39

4   6   7   9

6	x	9	–	4	+	7	=	57
	■		■		■		■	■
		7					=	12
	■		■		■		■	■
			6				=	27
	■		■		■		■	■
							=	32
=	■	=	■	=	■	=	■	■
23	■	72	■	37	■	13	■	■

33

Total Concentration

The blank squares below should be filled with whole numbers between 1 and 30 inclusive, any of which may occur more than once, or not at all. The numbers in every horizontal row add up to the totals on the right, as do the two long diagonal lines; whilst those in every vertical column add up to the totals along the bottom.

40

							81
20	2		6		24		103
5	14	1	30			21	88
6		23	17	21	27		136
11	4		20	5		9	75
	24	12		16	26	4	132
25		8		30	25	18	115
15	27	29	26	8			127
104	102	124	134	109	118	85	137

Symbol Sums

Each symbol stands for a different number. In order to reach the correct total at the end of each row and column, what is the value of the circle, pentagon, square and star?

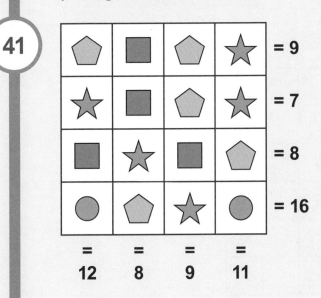

= 9
= 7
= 8
= 16

=
12
=
8
=
9
=
11

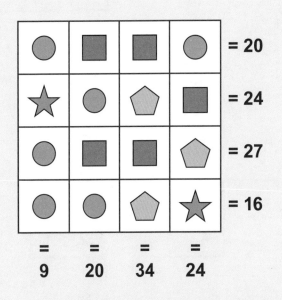

= 20
= 24
= 27
= 16

=
9
=
20
=
34
=
24

Tile Twister

Place the eight tiles into the puzzle grid so that all adjacent numbers on each tile match up. Tiles may be rotated through 360 degrees, but none may be flipped over.

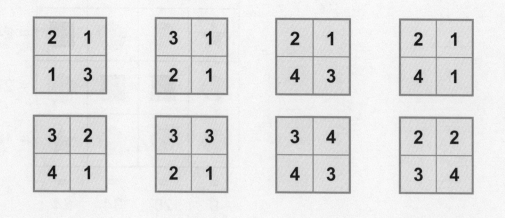

What's the Number?

In the diagram below, what number should replace the question mark?

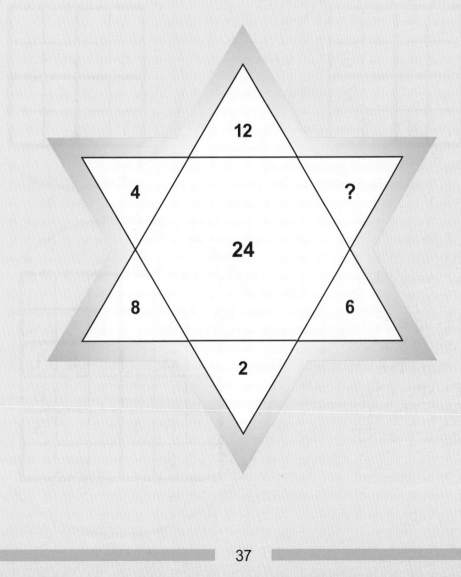

Mini Sudoku

Every row, every column and each of the four smaller boxes of four squares should be filled with a different number from 1 to 4 inclusive. Some numbers are already in place. Can you complete the grid?

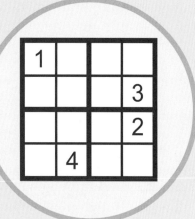

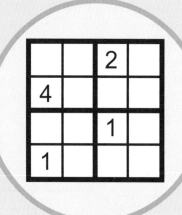

Every row, every column and each of the six smaller boxes of six squares should be filled with a different number from 1 to 6 inclusive. Some numbers are already in place. Can you complete the grid?

Sum Circle

Fill the three empty circles with the symbols +, – and x in some order, to make a sum which totals the number in the middle. Each symbol must be used once and calculations are made in the direction of travel (clockwise).

48

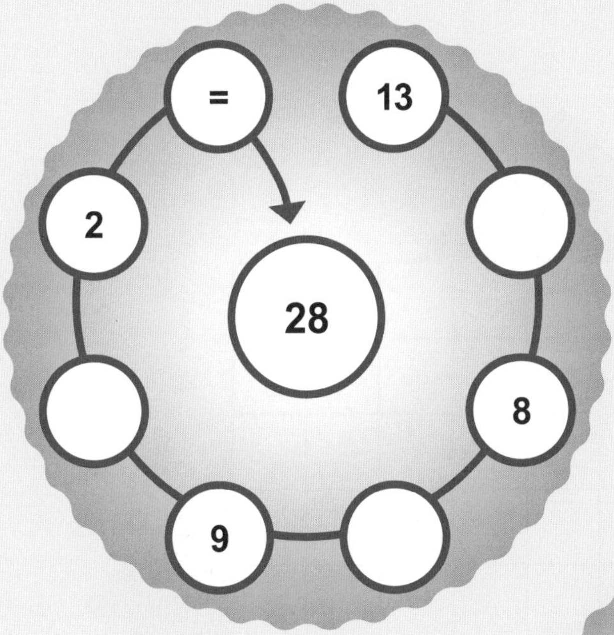

= 13

2

28

8

9

49

= 11

5

33

8

2

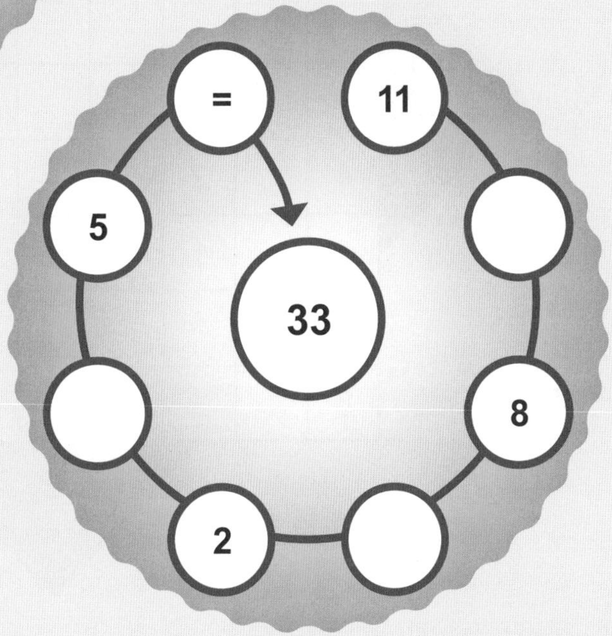

Number Path

Working from one square to another, horizontally or vertically (never diagonally), draw paths to pair up each set of two matching numbers. No path may be shared, and none may enter a square containing a number or part of another path.

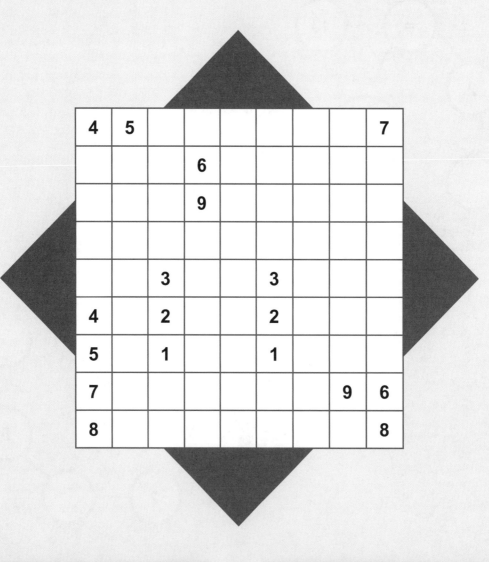

Hexagony

Can you place the hexagons into the grid, so that where any hexagon touches another along a straight line, the number in both triangles is the same? No rotation of any hexagon is allowed!

Number Crunch

Starting at the top left with the number provided, work down from one box to another, applying the mathematical instructions to your running total.

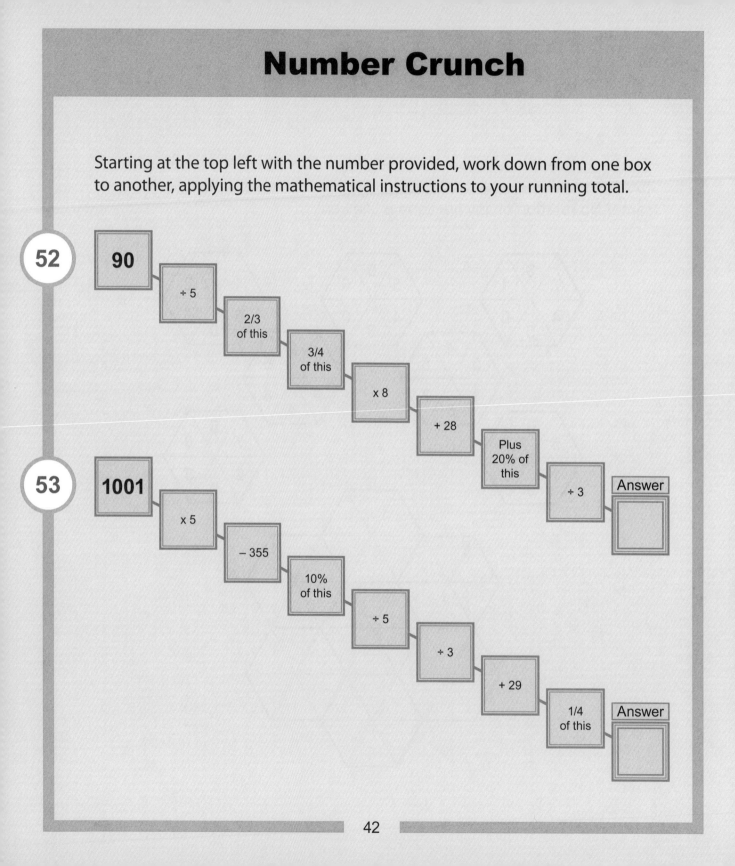

52

90

÷ 5

2/3 of this

3/4 of this

x 8

+ 28

Plus 20% of this

÷ 3

Answer

53

1001

x 5

− 355

10% of this

÷ 5

÷ 3

+ 29

1/4 of this

Answer

Pyramid Plus

The number in each circle is the sum of the two numbers below it. Just work out the missing numbers in every circle!

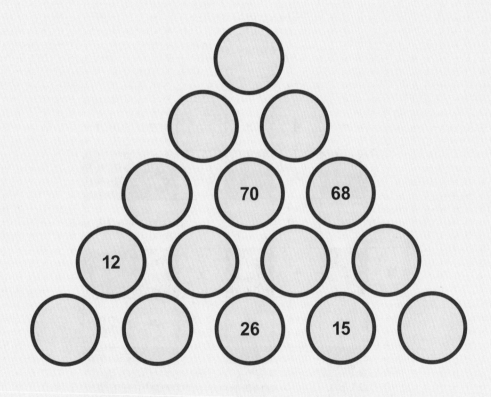

One to Nine

Using the numbers one to nine, complete these six equations (three reading across and three reading downwards). Every number is used once only, and one is already in place.

55

1 2 3 4 5 6 7 8 9

	+	4	x		=	63
−		x		+		
	x		−		=	26
x		+		x		
	x		+		=	20
=		=		=		
4		42		64		

Summing Up

Arrange one of each of the four given numbers, as well as one each of the symbols – (minus), x (times) and + (plus) in every row and column to arrive at the answer at the end of the row or column, making the calculations in the order in which they appear. Some are already in place.

2   4   5   8

2	+	8	x	5	–	4	=	46
	■		■		■		■	■
							=	26
	■		■		■		■	■
4							=	43
	■	x			■		■	■
							=	42
=	■	=	■	=	■	=	■	■
14	■	30	■	28	■	58	■	■

45

Total Concentration

The blank squares below should be filled with whole numbers between 1 and 30 inclusive, any of which may occur more than once, or not at all. The numbers in every horizontal row add up to the totals on the right, as do the two long diagonal lines; whilst those in every vertical column add up to the totals along the bottom.

57

								94
	27	25	10		17	13	118	
	3	24	16		10	23	109	
18		30	16	19		23	144	
14	24	5		2	26		111	
4	15	15	27	9			101	
28	12		20		21	25	113	
			8	20	22	7	111	
98	112	121	108	95	135	138	90	

Symbol Sums

Each symbol stands for a different number. In order to reach the correct total at the end of each row and column, what is the value of the circle, pentagon, square and star?

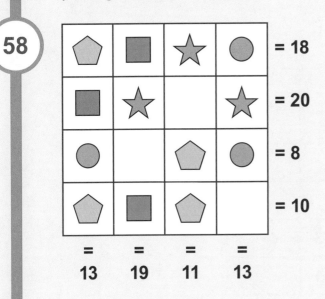

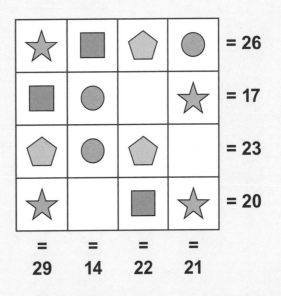

Tile Twister

Place the eight tiles into the puzzle grid so that all adjacent numbers on each tile match up. Tiles may be rotated through 360 degrees, but none may be flipped over.

60

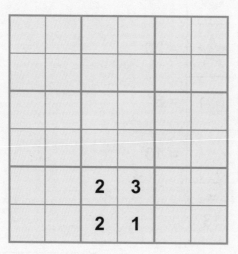

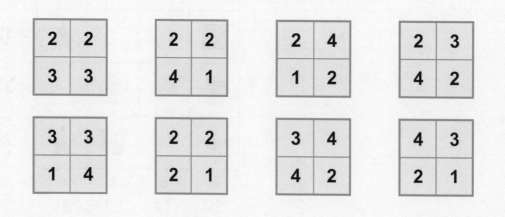

What's the Number?

In the diagram below, what number should replace the question mark?

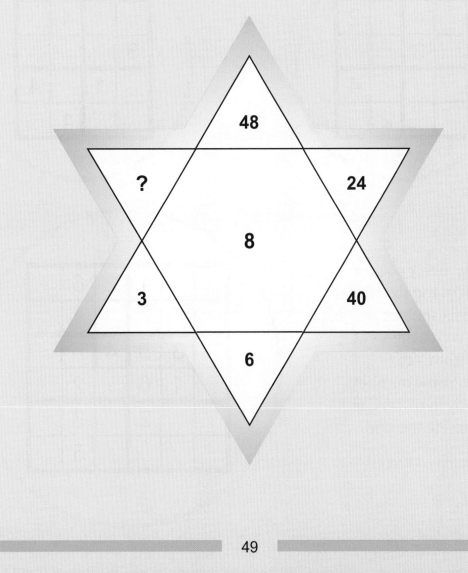

Mini Sudoku

Every row, every column and each of the four smaller boxes of four squares should be filled with a different number from 1 to 4 inclusive. Some numbers are already in place. Can you complete the grid?

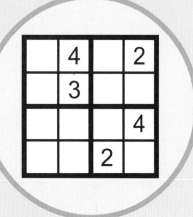

62

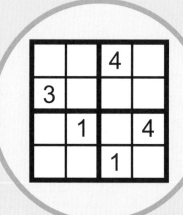

63

64

Every row, every column and each of the six smaller boxes of six squares should be filled with a different number from 1 to 6 inclusive. Some numbers are already in place. Can you complete the grid?

Sum Circle

Fill the three empty circles with the symbols +, – and x in some order, to make a sum which totals the number in the middle. Each symbol must be used once and calculations are made in the direction of travel (clockwise).

65

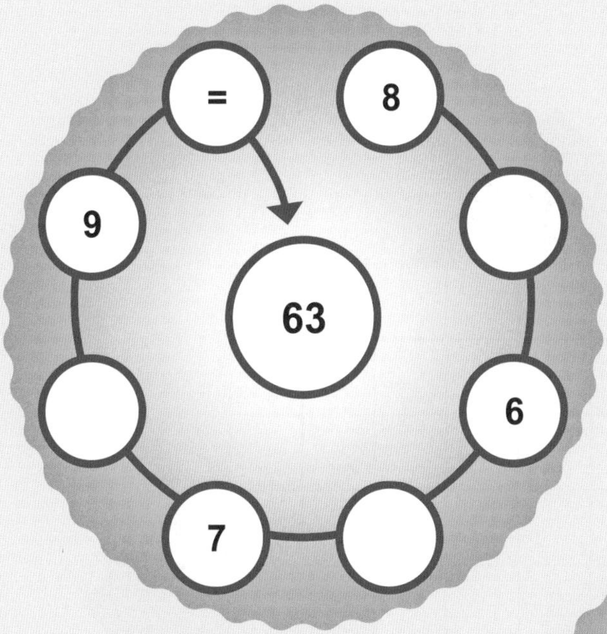

= 8 9 63 6 7

66

= 4 3 71 17 6

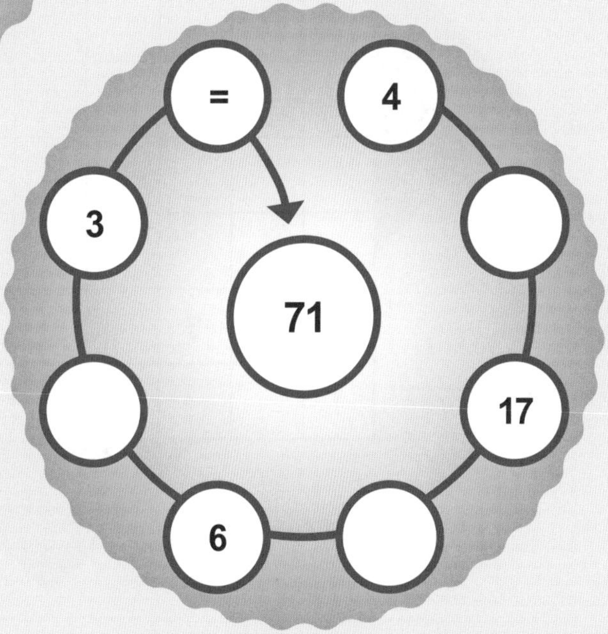

Number Path

Working from one square to another, horizontally or vertically (never diagonally), draw paths to pair up each set of two matching numbers. No path may be shared, and none may enter a square containing a number or part of another path.

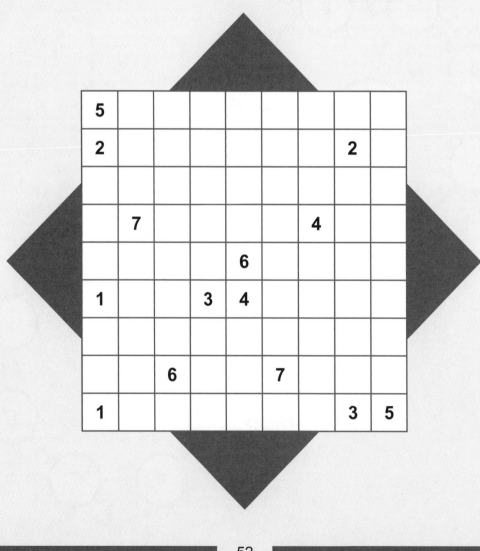

Hexagony

Can you place the hexagons into the grid, so that where any hexagon touches another along a straight line, the number in both triangles is the same? No rotation of any hexagon is allowed!

Number Crunch

Starting at the top left with the number provided, work down from one box to another, applying the mathematical instructions to your running total.

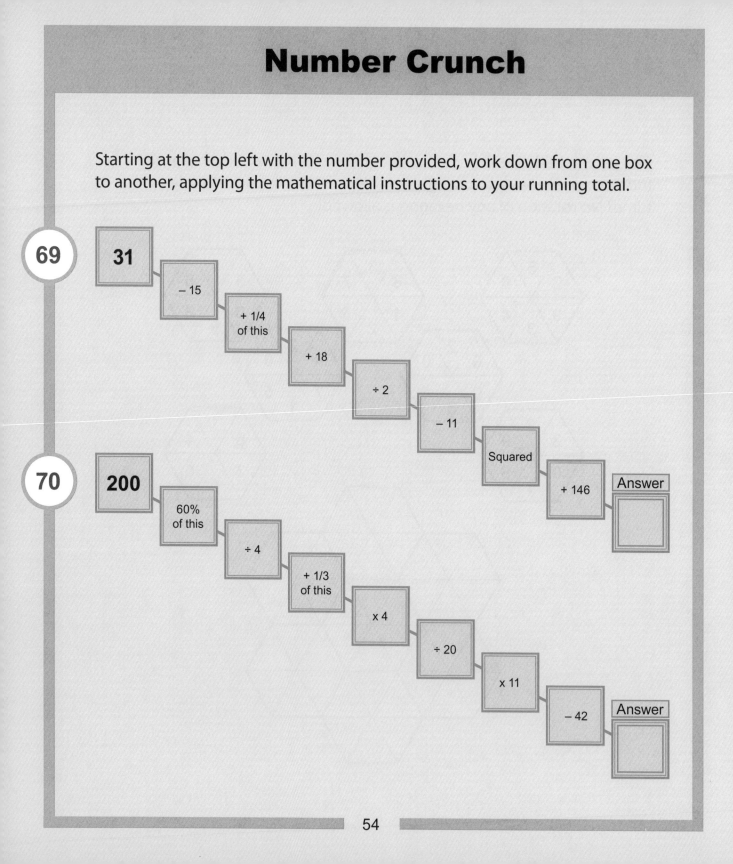

69

31 → − 15 → + 1/4 of this → + 18 → ÷ 2 → − 11 → Squared → + 146 → Answer

70

200 → 60% of this → ÷ 4 → + 1/3 of this → x 4 → ÷ 20 → x 11 → − 42 → Answer

Pyramid Plus

The number in each circle is the sum of the two numbers below it. Just work out the missing numbers in every circle!

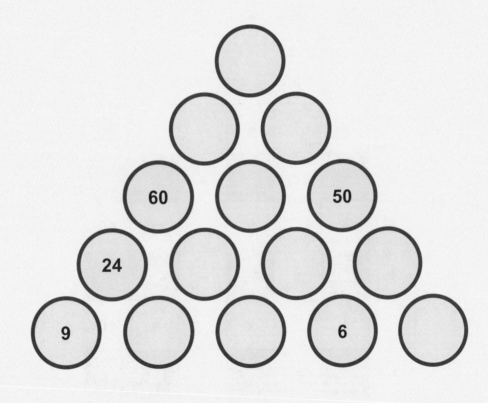

One to Nine

Using the numbers one to nine, complete these six equations (three reading across and three reading downwards). Every number is used once only, and one is already in place.

1 2 3 4 5 6 7 8 9

	x		+		=	30
−		+		x		
5	+		x		=	49
+		x		−		
	+		x		=	40
=		=		=		
4		45		38		

Summing Up

Arrange one of each of the four given numbers, as well as one each of the symbols – (minus), x (times) and + (plus) in every row and column to arrive at the answer at the end of the row or column, making the calculations in the order in which they appear. Some are already in place.

73

3   6   7   9

3	+	7	–	9	x	6	=	6
x								
							=	43
				–				
							=	58
7				3	x		=	36
=		=		=		=		
26		42		24		48		

Total Concentration

The blank squares below should be filled with whole numbers between 1 and 30 inclusive, any of which may occur more than once, or not at all. The numbers in every horizontal row add up to the totals on the right, as do the two long diagonal lines; whilst those in every vertical column add up to the totals along the bottom.

							47
11		2	15	29		5	78
30	21		4	24	1		101
	12	23	20		8	25	103
	28	10		1	13	7	84
7		19	14	17	26		102
	2	13		28	5	16	103
6	8	28	18			27	116
110	93	104	83	125	77	95	107

Symbol Sums

Each symbol stands for a different number. In order to reach the correct total at the end of each row and column, what is the value of the circle, pentagon, square and star?

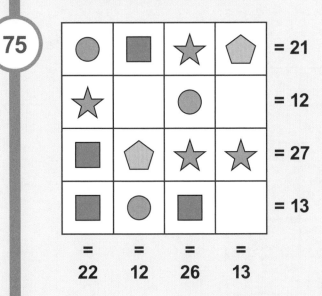

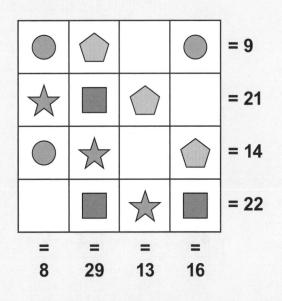

59

Tile Twister

Place the eight tiles into the puzzle grid so that all adjacent numbers on each tile match up. Tiles may be rotated through 360 degrees, but none may be flipped over.

77

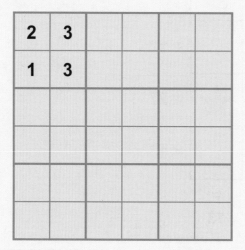

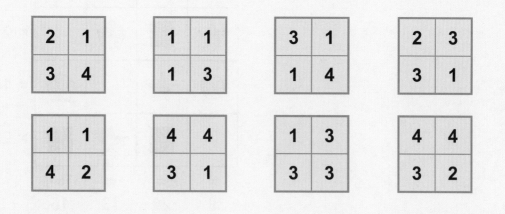

What's the Number?

In the diagram below, what number should replace the question mark?

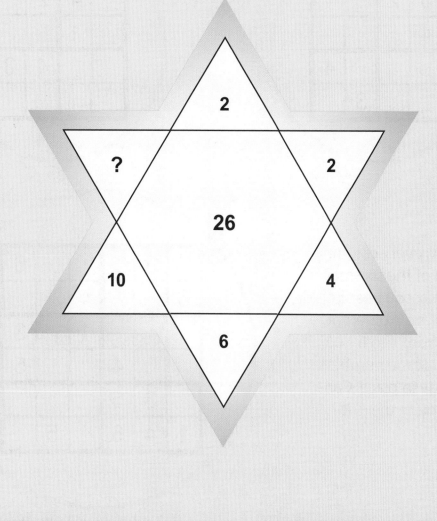

Mini Sudoku

Every row, every column and each of the four smaller boxes of four squares should be filled with a different number from 1 to 4 inclusive. Some numbers are already in place. Can you complete the grid?

79

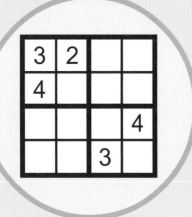

80

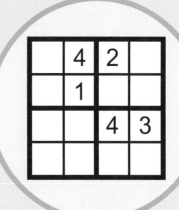

81

Every row, every column and each of the six smaller boxes of six squares should be filled with a different number from 1 to 6 inclusive. Some numbers are already in place. Can you complete the grid?

Sum Circle

Fill the three empty circles with the symbols +, – and x in some order, to make a sum which totals the number in the middle. Each symbol must be used once and calculations are made in the direction of travel (clockwise).

82

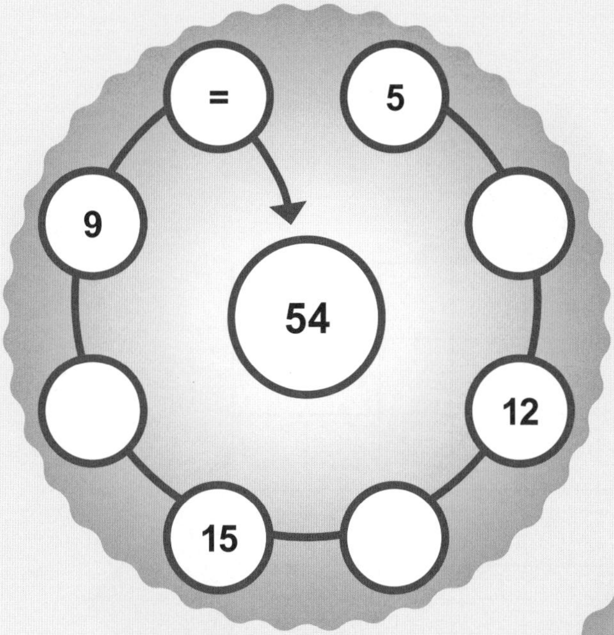

= 5

9

54

12

15

83

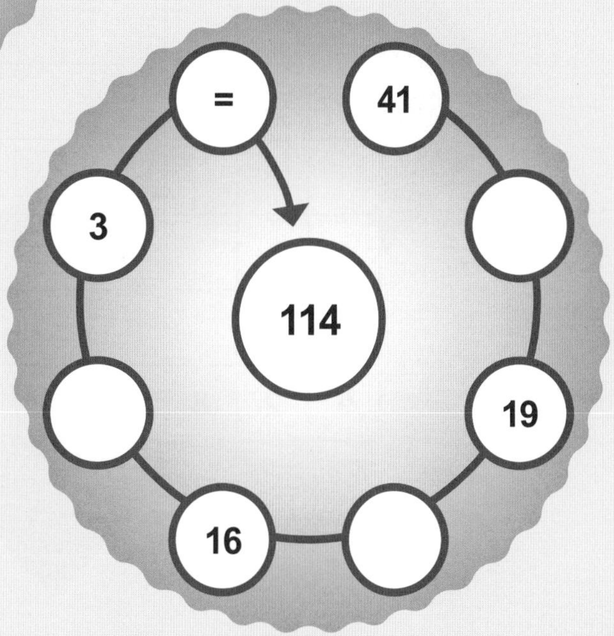

= 41

3

114

19

16

Number Path

Working from one square to another, horizontally or vertically (never diagonally), draw paths to pair up each set of two matching numbers. No path may be shared, and none may enter a square containing a number or part of another path.

84

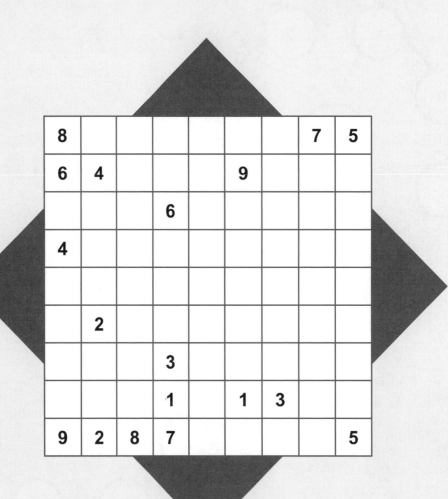

Hexagony

Can you place the hexagons into the grid, so that where any hexagon touches another along a straight line, the number in both triangles is the same? No rotation of any hexagon is allowed!

Number Crunch

Starting at the top left with the number provided, work down from one box to another, applying the mathematical instructions to your running total.

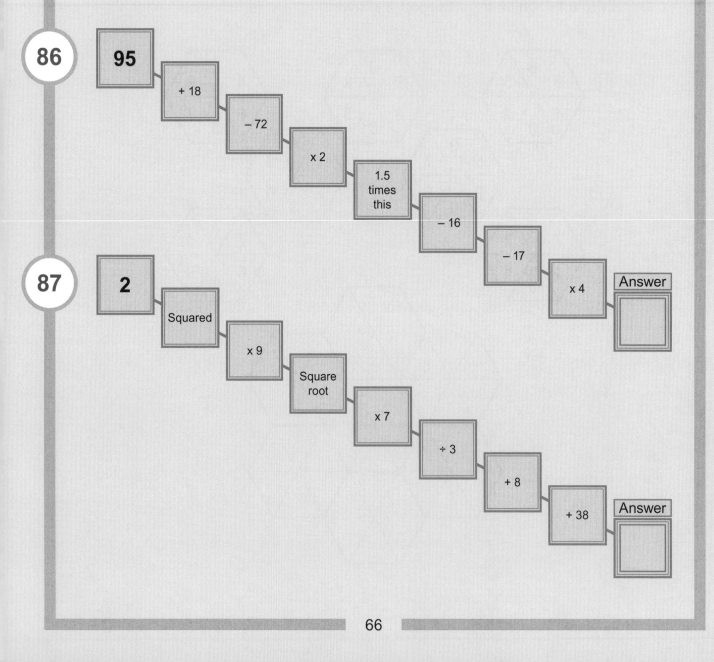

86

95 → + 18 → − 72 → x 2 → 1.5 times this → − 16 → − 17 → x 4 → Answer

87

2 → Squared → x 9 → Square root → x 7 → ÷ 3 → + 8 → + 38 → Answer

Pyramid Plus

The number in each circle is the sum of the two numbers below it. Just work out the missing numbers in every circle!

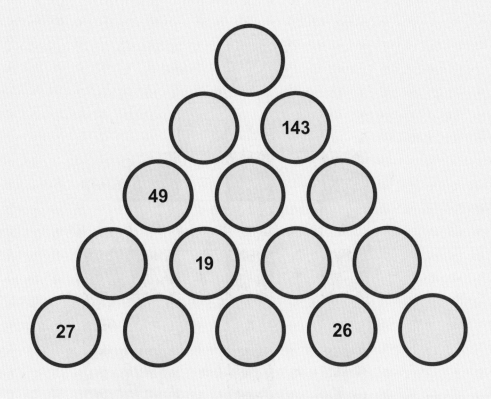

One to Nine

Using the numbers one to nine, complete these six equations (three reading across and three reading downwards). Every number is used once only, and one is already in place.

89

1 2 3 4 5 6 7 8 9

	+		x		=	30
+		x		−		
6	+		−		=	12
−		+		x		
	−		x		=	49
=		=		=		
2		19		14		

Summing Up

Arrange one of each of the four given numbers, as well as one each of the symbols – (minus), x (times) and + (plus) in every row and column to arrive at the answer at the end of the row or column, making the calculations in the order in which they appear. Some are already in place.

3   4   6   8

6	+	4	x	8	–	3	=	77
							=	26
x								
	–				+		=	14
				3			=	44
=		=		=		=		
20		30		27		22		

69

Total Concentration

91

The blank squares below should be filled with whole numbers between 1 and 30 inclusive, any of which may occur more than once, or not at all. The numbers in every horizontal row add up to the totals on the right, as do the two long diagonal lines; whilst those in every vertical column add up to the totals along the bottom.

							102
5			6	14	25	26	120
7	15	24			5	13	107
	4	3		23	4	26	93
11	21	22			19		110
28		17	3	27		8	127
	2		29	30	23	30	126
28	18	29	9		19		126
102	97	132	78	157	119	124	75

Symbol Sums

Each symbol stands for a different number. In order to reach the correct total at the end of each row and column, what is the value of the circle, pentagon, square and star?

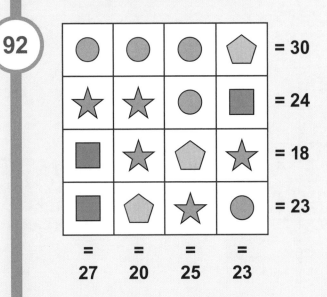

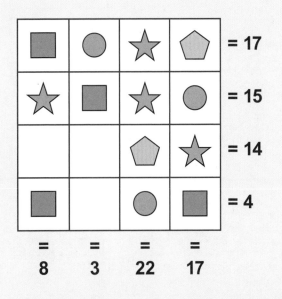

71

Tile Twister

Place the eight tiles into the puzzle grid so that all adjacent numbers on each tile match up. Tiles may be rotated through 360 degrees, but none may be flipped over.

94

				2	4
				4	1

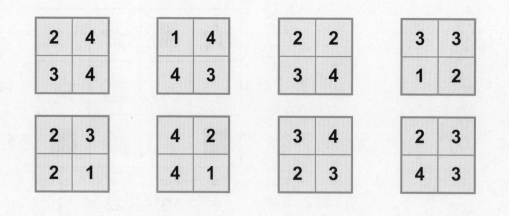

72

What's the Number?

In the diagram below, what number should replace the question mark?

95

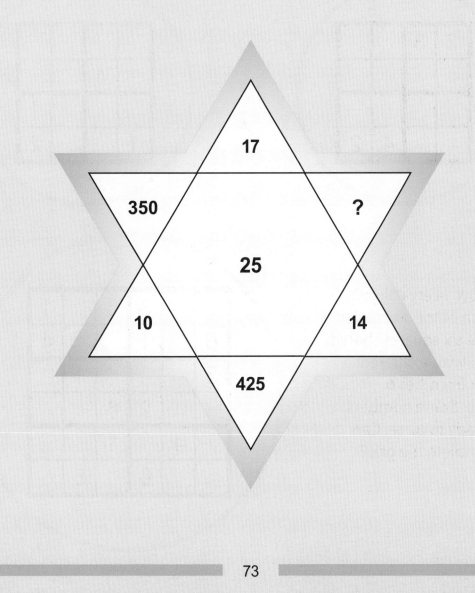

Mini Sudoku

Every row, every column and each of the four smaller boxes of four squares should be filled with a different number from 1 to 4 inclusive. Some numbers are already in place. Can you complete the grid?

96

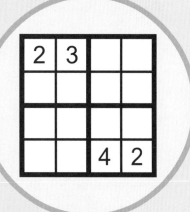

97

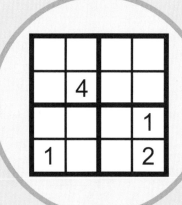

98

Every row, every column and each of the six smaller boxes of six squares should be filled with a different number from 1 to 6 inclusive. Some numbers are already in place. Can you complete the grid?

		3	5		1
6		1			4
3				1	
		2	6		
	4		1		
		6		5	

Sum Circle

Fill the three empty circles with the symbols +, – and x in some order, to make a sum which totals the number in the middle. Each symbol must be used once and calculations are made in the direction of travel (clockwise).

99

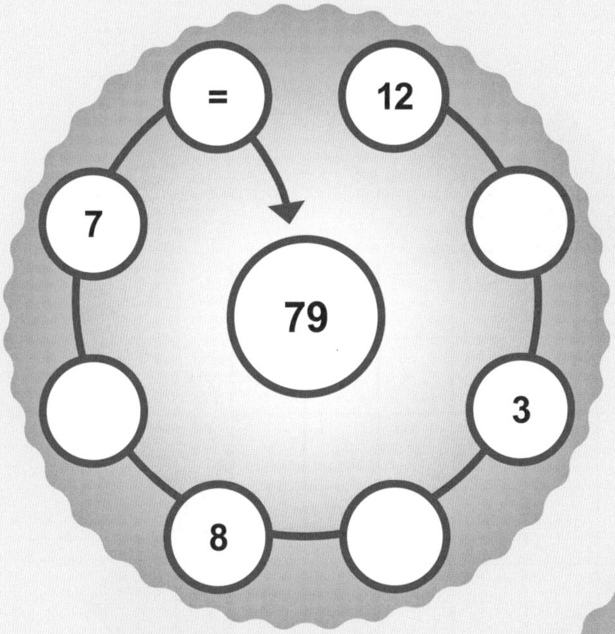

= 12

7

79

3

8

100

= 18

4

132

13

28

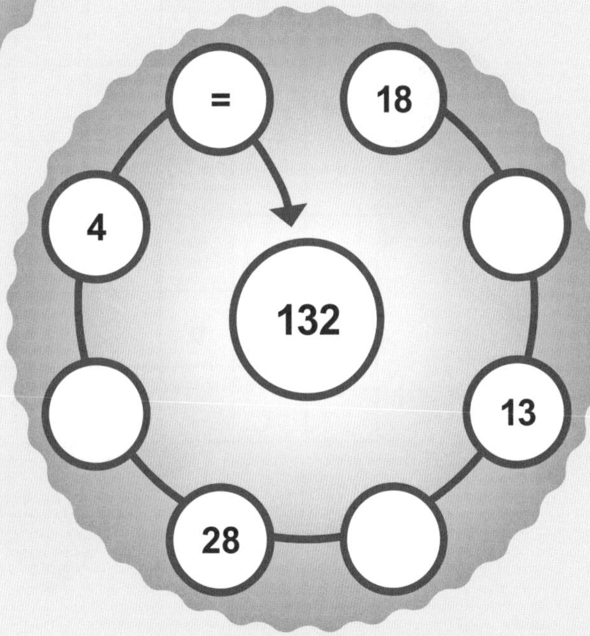

Number Path

Working from one square to another, horizontally or vertically (never diagonally), draw paths to pair up each set of two matching numbers. No path may be shared, and none may enter a square containing a number or part of another path.

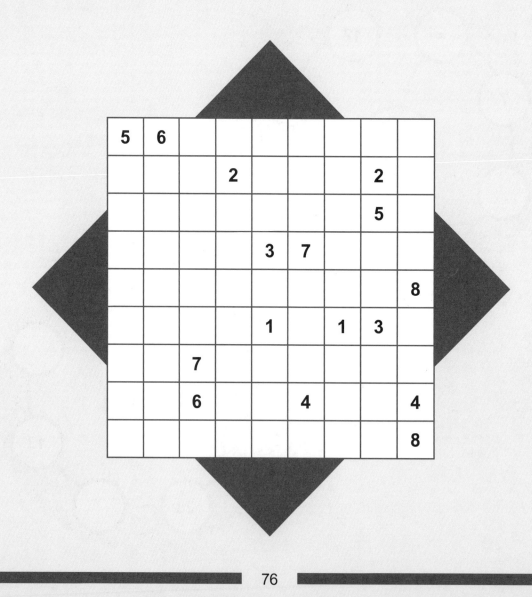

Hexagony

Can you place the hexagons into the grid, so that where any hexagon touches another along a straight line, the number in both triangles is the same? No rotation of any hexagon is allowed!

Number Crunch

Starting at the top left with the number provided, work down from one box to another, applying the mathematical instructions to your running total.

103

35

÷ 5

+ 27

x 2

÷ 4

− 8

Square root

x 15

Answer

104

67

− 22

÷ 9

Squared

x 5

+ 25

10% of this

+ 29

Answer

Pyramid Plus

The number in each circle is the sum of the two numbers below it. Just work out the missing numbers in every circle!

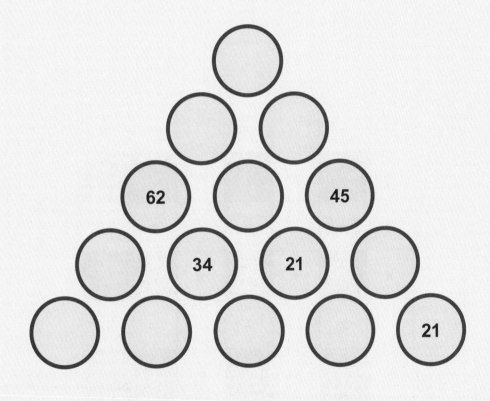

One to Nine

Using the numbers one to nine, complete these six equations (three reading across and three reading downwards). Every number is used once only, and one is already in place.

106

1 2 3 4 5 6 7 8 9

	−		x		=	8
+		x		+		
1	+		x		=	36
x		+		x		
	x		−		=	33
=		=		=		
45		25		26		

Summing Up

Arrange one of each of the four given numbers, as well as one each of the symbols – (minus), x (times) and + (plus) in every row and column to arrive at the answer at the end of the row or column, making the calculations in the order in which they appear. Some are already in place.

2 5 7 9

5	+	9	x	2	–	7	=	21
	■		■		■		■	■
							=	12
	■		■		■		■	■
				9			=	50
	■		■		■		■	■
					x		=	22
=	■	=	■	=	■	=	■	■
90		15		76		78	■	■

107

Total Concentration

The blank squares below should be filled with whole numbers between 1 and 30 inclusive, any of which may occur more than once, or not at all. The numbers in every horizontal row add up to the totals on the right, as do the two long diagonal lines; whilst those in every vertical column add up to the totals along the bottom.

108

							110
	19	26		18	20	16	110
25			14	15	9	21	97
18	27	8	19	4			106
7	24		8	22	14		90
		20	23	2	17	12	111
21	23	29	10			1	108
	15	22		16	11	24	128
135	123	124	89	90	99	90	65

Symbol Sums

Each symbol stands for a different number. In order to reach the correct total at the end of each row and column, what is the value of the circle, pentagon, square and star?

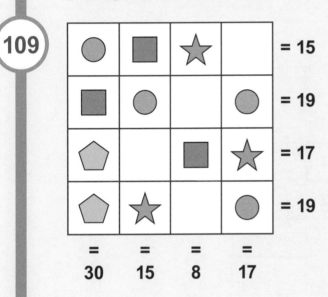

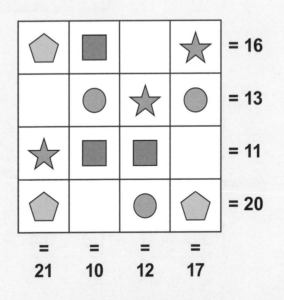

83

Tile Twister

Place the eight tiles into the puzzle grid so that all adjacent numbers on each tile match up. Tiles may be rotated through 360 degrees, but none may be flipped over.

111

		4	4		
		4	2		

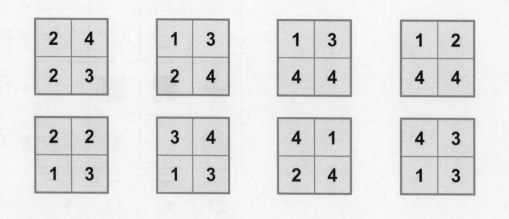

2	4
2	3

1	3
2	4

1	3
4	4

1	2
4	4

2	2
1	3

3	4
1	3

4	1
2	4

4	3
1	3

What's the Number?

In the diagram below, what number should replace the question mark?

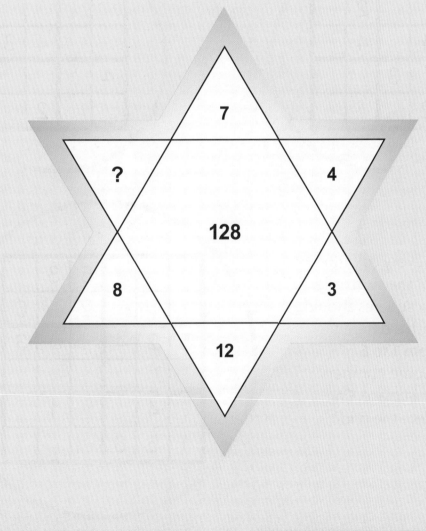

Mini Sudoku

Every row, every column and each of the four smaller boxes of four squares should be filled with a different number from 1 to 4 inclusive. Some numbers are already in place. Can you complete the grid?

113

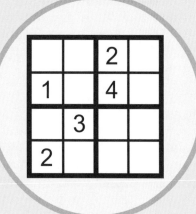

114

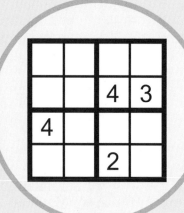

115

Every row, every column and each of the six smaller boxes of six squares should be filled with a different number from 1 to 6 inclusive. Some numbers are already in place. Can you complete the grid?

Sum Circle

Fill the three empty circles with the symbols +, – and x in some order, to make a sum which totals the number in the middle. Each symbol must be used once and calculations are made in the direction of travel (clockwise).

116

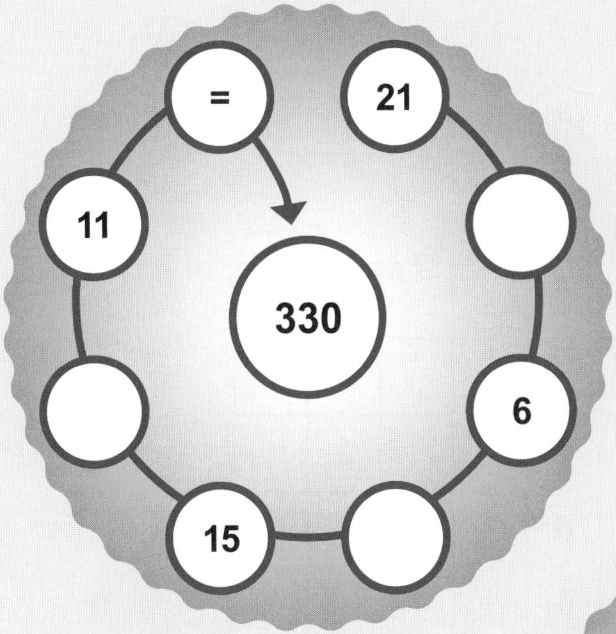

= 21

11

330

6

15

117

= 18

6

126

7

4

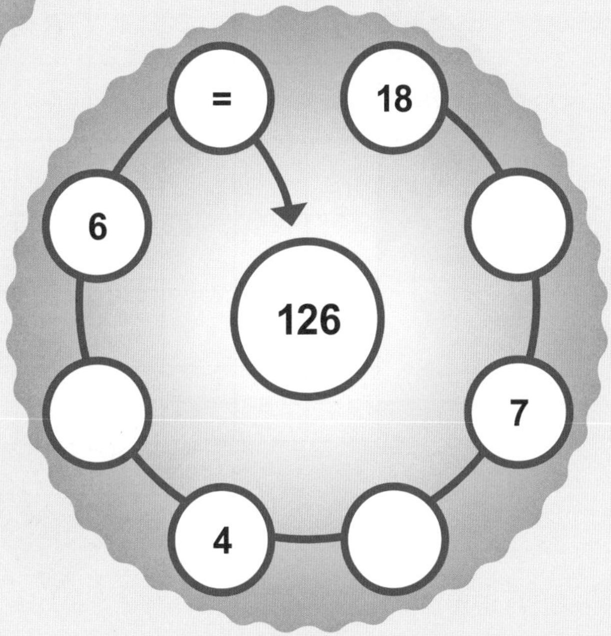

Number Path

Working from one square to another, horizontally or vertically (never diagonally), draw paths to pair up each set of two matching numbers. No path may be shared, and none may enter a square containing a number or part of another path.

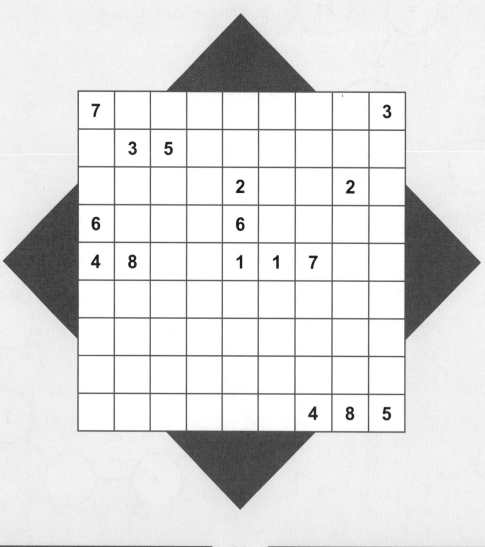

Hexagony

Can you place the hexagons into the grid, so that where any hexagon touches another along a straight line, the number in both triangles is the same? No rotation of any hexagon is allowed!

Number Crunch

Starting at the top left with the number provided, work down from one box to another, applying the mathematical instructions to your running total.

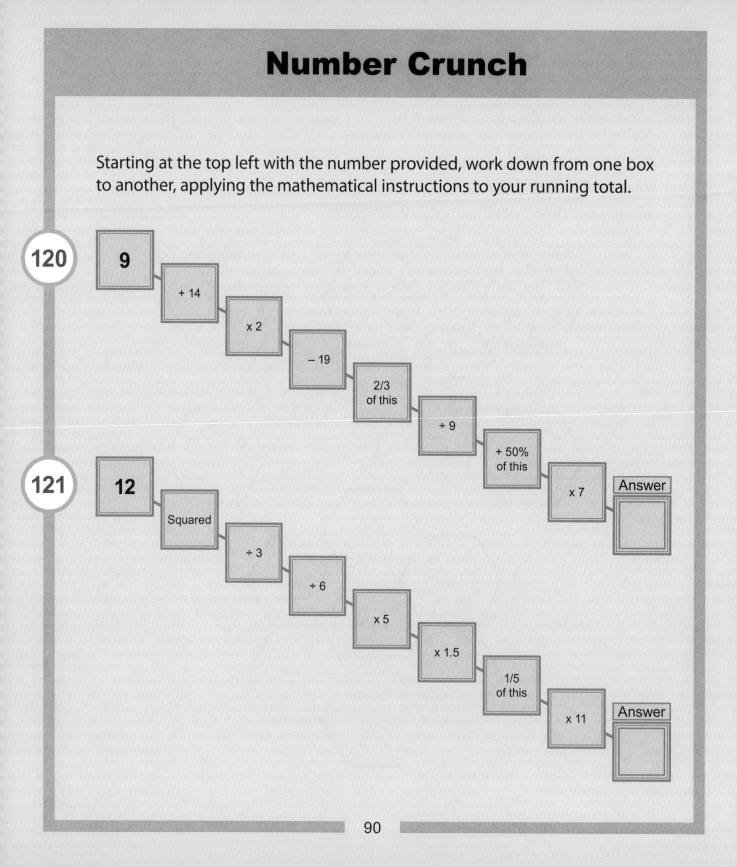

120

9
+ 14
x 2
− 19
2/3 of this
÷ 9
+ 50% of this
x 7
Answer

121

12
Squared
÷ 3
÷ 6
x 5
x 1.5
1/5 of this
x 11
Answer

Pyramid Plus

The number in each circle is the sum of the two numbers below it. Just work out the missing numbers in every circle!

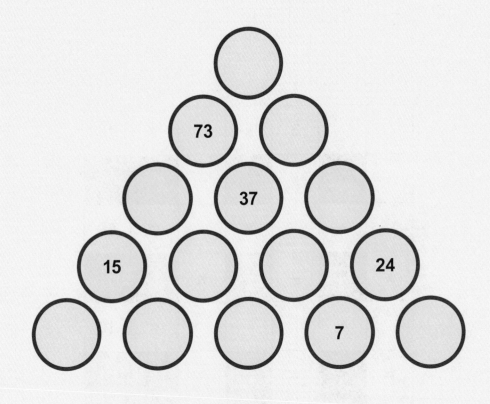

One to Nine

Using the numbers one to nine, complete these six equations (three reading across and three reading downwards). Every number is used once only, and one is already in place.

123

1 2 3 4 5 6 7 8 9

	−	3	x		=	48
+		x		−		
	+		x		=	40
x		−		x		
	+		−		=	10
=		=		=		
77		14		3		

Summing Up

Arrange one of each of the four given numbers, as well as one each of the symbols – (minus), x (times) and + (plus) in every row and column to arrive at the answer at the end of the row or column, making the calculations in the order in which they appear. Some are already in place.

3   4   7   8

4	+	7	x	3	–	8	=	25
	■		■		■		■	
				7			=	39
	■		■		■		■	
	x				+		=	11
	■				■		■	
			+				=	57
=	■	=	■	=	■	=	■	
36	■	24	■	76	■	33	■	

93

Total Concentration

The blank squares below should be filled with whole numbers between 1 and 30 inclusive, any of which may occur more than once, or not at all. The numbers in every horizontal row add up to the totals on the right, as do the two long diagonal lines; whilst those in every vertical column add up to the totals along the bottom.

125

							69
13			18	12	26	30	112
3		2	9	19	4		82
27	11		1	17	8	22	111
20	6	21	11	29			107
12	28	2				10	117
	4	13		24	9	6	68
	8	7			26	25	124
83	89	80	99	145	101	124	126

Symbol Sums

Each symbol stands for a different number. In order to reach the correct total at the end of each row and column, what is the value of the circle, pentagon, square and star?

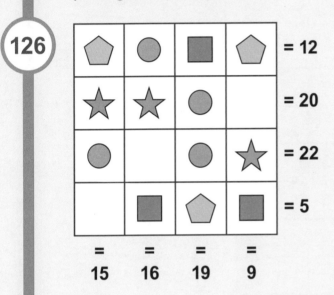

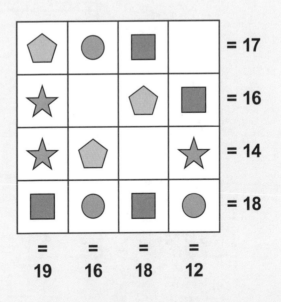

Tile Twister

Place the eight tiles into the puzzle grid so that all adjacent numbers on each tile match up. Tiles may be rotated through 360 degrees, but none may be flipped over.

128

		1	3		
		2	3		

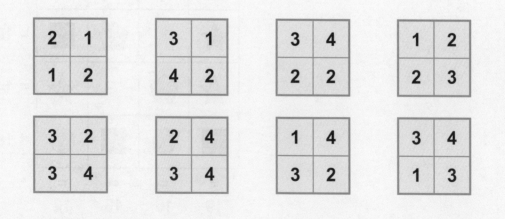

2	1
1	2

3	1
4	2

3	4
2	2

1	2
2	3

3	2
3	4

2	4
3	4

1	4
3	2

3	4
1	3

What's the Number?

In the diagram below, what number should replace the question mark?

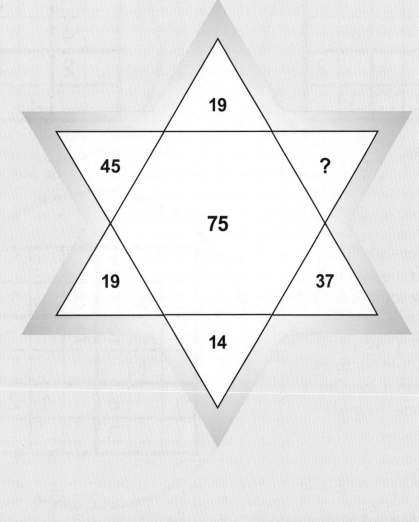

Mini Sudoku

Every row, every column and each of the four smaller boxes of four squares should be filled with a different number from 1 to 4 inclusive. Some numbers are already in place. Can you complete the grid?

130

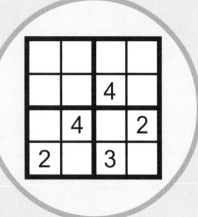

131

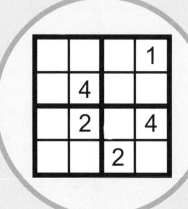

132

Every row, every column and each of the six smaller boxes of six squares should be filled with a different number from 1 to 6 inclusive. Some numbers are already in place. Can you complete the grid?

Sum Circle

Fill the three empty circles with the symbols +, – and x in some order, to make a sum which totals the number in the middle. Each symbol must be used once and calculations are made in the direction of travel (clockwise).

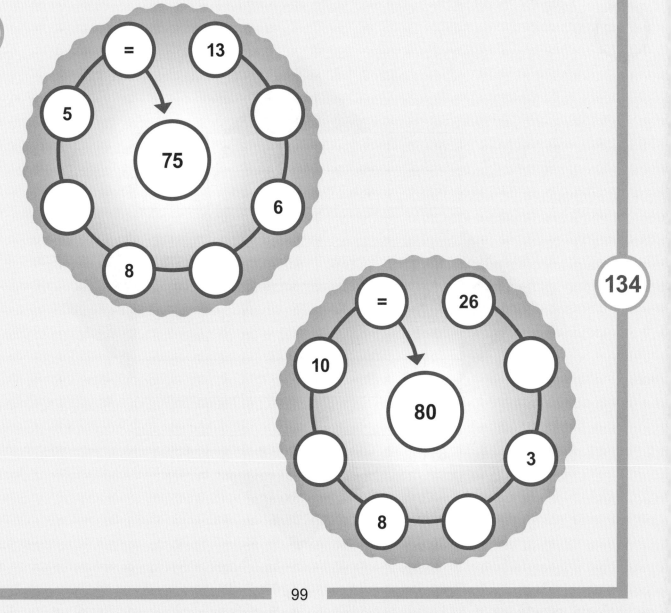

Number Path

Working from one square to another, horizontally or vertically (never diagonally), draw paths to pair up each set of two matching numbers. No path may be shared, and none may enter a square containing a number or part of another path.

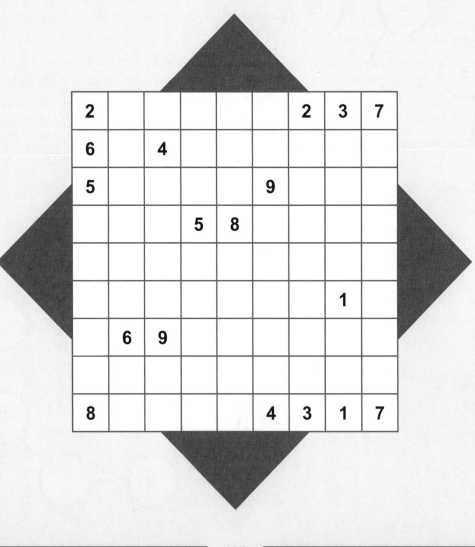

Hexagony

Can you place the hexagons into the grid, so that where any hexagon touches another along a straight line, the number in both triangles is the same? No rotation of any hexagon is allowed!

Number Crunch

Starting at the top left with the number provided, work down from one box to another, applying the mathematical instructions to your running total.

137

85 → 1/5 of this → x 2 → + 8 → x 2 → ÷ 7 → + 88 → 24% of this → Answer

138

2006 → − 1008 → ÷ 2 → − 9 → ÷ 70 → x 3 → + 8 → x 2 → Answer

Pyramid Plus

The number in each circle is the sum of the two numbers below it. Just work out the missing numbers in every circle!

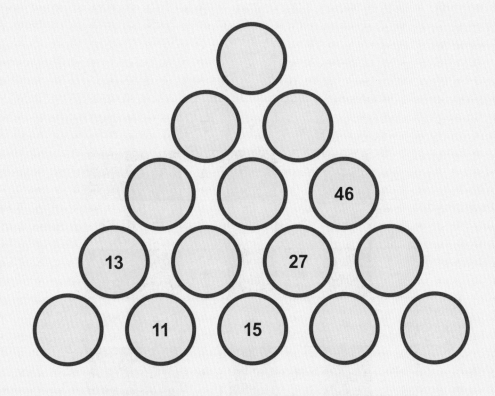

One to Nine

Using the numbers one to nine, complete these six equations (three reading across and three reading downwards). Every number is used once only, and one is already in place.

1 2 3 4 5 6 7 8 9

	+		x	7	=	35
x		+		−		
	+		−		=	12
−		x		+		
	x		+		=	24
=		=		=		
21		45		14		

Summing Up

Arrange one of each of the four given numbers, as well as one each of the symbols – (minus), x (times) and + (plus) in every row and column to arrive at the answer at the end of the row or column, making the calculations in the order in which they appear. Some are already in place.

2   5   6   8

5	x	8	+	2	–	6	=	36
							=	28
	–				x		=	18
						–		
			8			=	59	
=		=		=		=		
86		66		12		23		

105

Total Concentration

The blank squares below should be filled with whole numbers between 1 and 30 inclusive, any of which may occur more than once, or not at all. The numbers in every horizontal row add up to the totals on the right, as do the two long diagonal lines; whilst those in every vertical column add up to the totals along the bottom.

142

							121
20	1	22		1		21	101
23			15	24	17	30	126
3		13	16		6	21	98
12			5	14	29		139
	4	11	26	26		7	111
29	25	18			28	18	155
19	10	27	2		8		112
123	101	117	87	135	130	149	134

Symbol Sums

Each symbol stands for a different number. In order to reach the correct total at the end of each row and column, what is the value of the circle, pentagon, square and star?

143

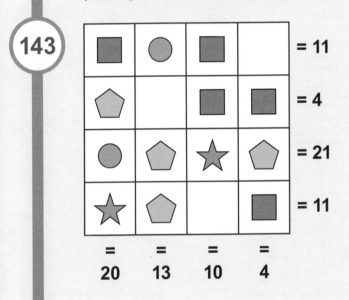

144

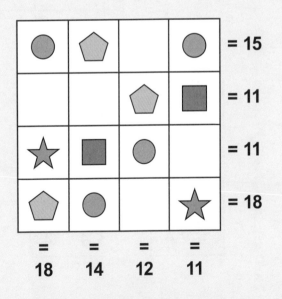

Tile Twister

Place the eight tiles into the puzzle grid so that all adjacent numbers on each tile match up. Tiles may be rotated through 360 degrees, but none may be flipped over.

145

2	4				
2	3				

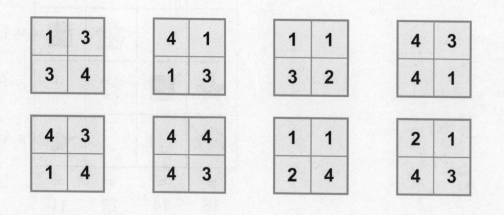

1	3
3	4

4	1
1	3

1	1
3	2

4	3
4	1

4	3
1	4

4	4
4	3

1	1
2	4

2	1
4	3

What's the Number?

In the diagram below, what number should replace the question mark?

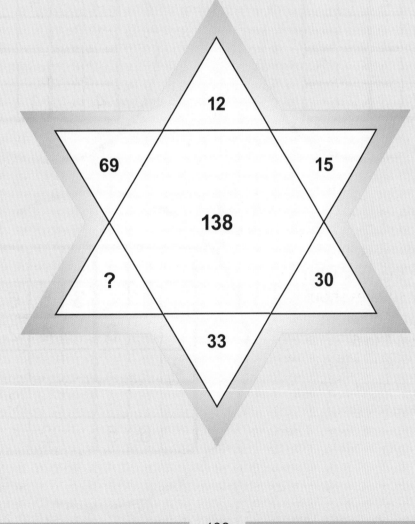

Mini Sudoku

Every row, every column and each of the four smaller boxes of four squares should be filled with a different number from 1 to 4 inclusive. Some numbers are already in place. Can you complete the grid?

147

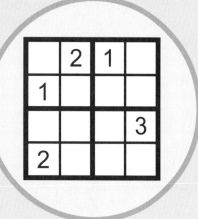

148

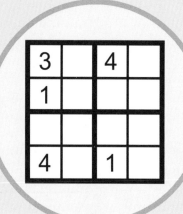

149

Every row, every column and each of the six smaller boxes of six squares should be filled with a different number from 1 to 6 inclusive. Some numbers are already in place. Can you complete the grid?

Sum Circle

Fill the three empty circles with the symbols +, – and x in some order, to make a sum which totals the number in the middle. Each symbol must be used once and calculations are made in the direction of travel (clockwise).

150

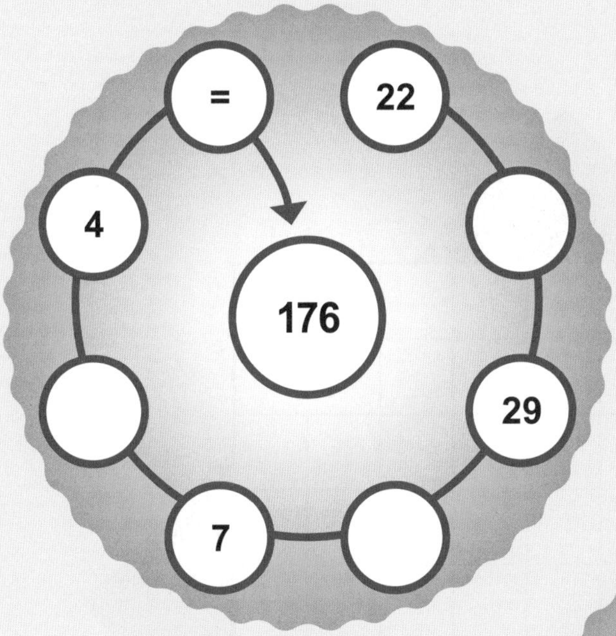

= 22

4

176

29

7

151

= 14

7

103

8

16

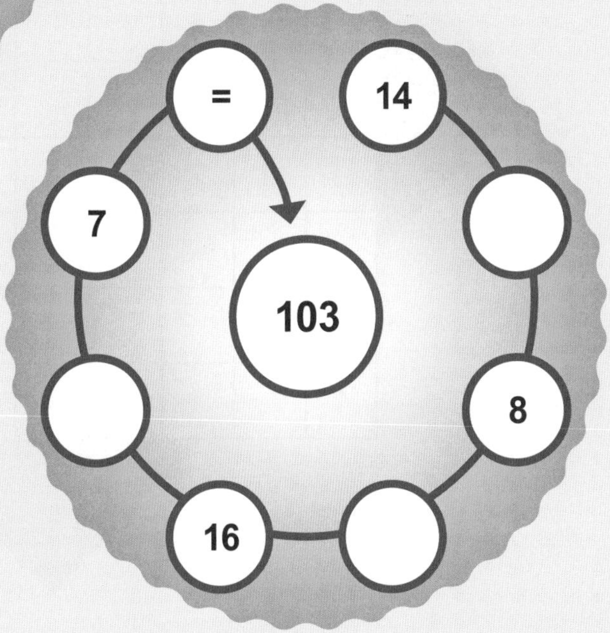

Number Path

Working from one square to another, horizontally or vertically (never diagonally), draw paths to pair up each set of two matching numbers. No path may be shared, and none may enter a square containing a number or part of another path.

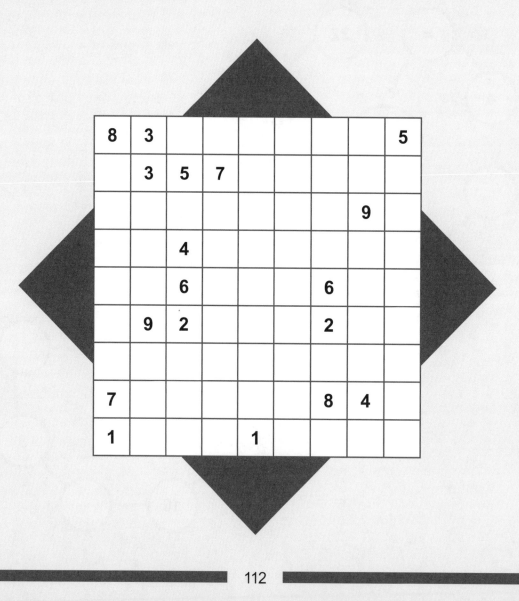

Hexagony

Can you place the hexagons into the grid, so that where any hexagon touches another along a straight line, the number in both triangles is the same? No rotation of any hexagon is allowed!

Number Crunch

Starting at the top left with the number provided, work down from one box to another, applying the mathematical instructions to your running total.

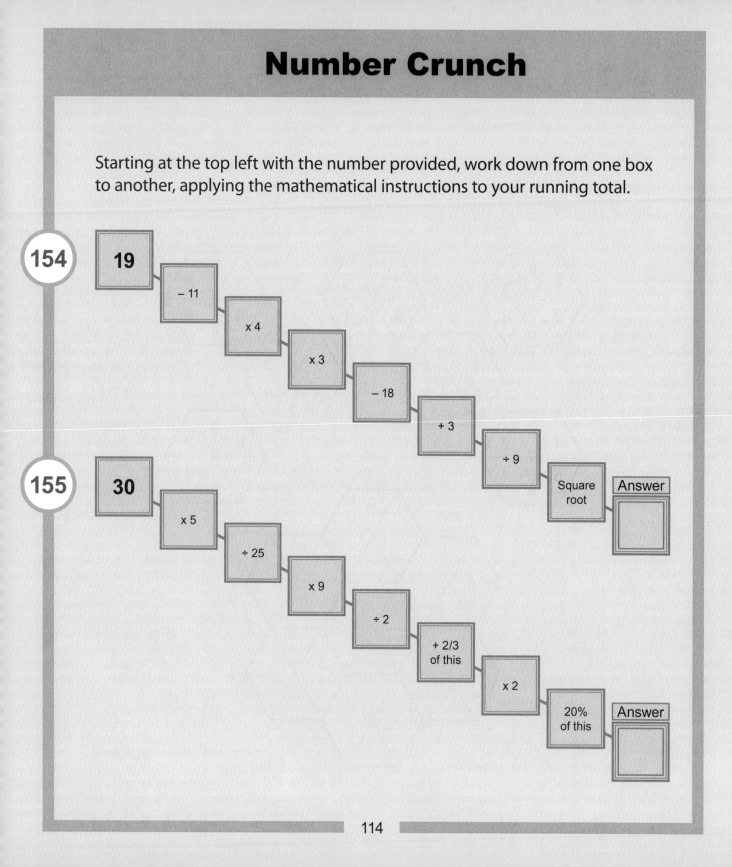

154

19

− 11

x 4

x 3

− 18

+ 3

÷ 9

Square root

Answer

155

30

x 5

÷ 25

x 9

÷ 2

+ 2/3 of this

x 2

20% of this

Answer

Pyramid Plus

The number in each circle is the sum of the two numbers below it. Just work out the missing numbers in every circle!

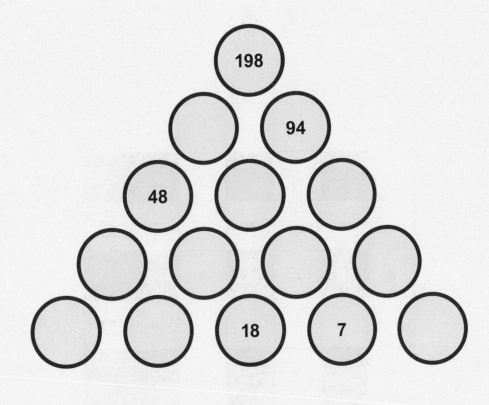

One to Nine

Using the numbers one to nine, complete these six equations (three reading across and three reading downwards). Every number is used once only, and one is already in place.

157

1 2 3 4 5 6 7 8 9

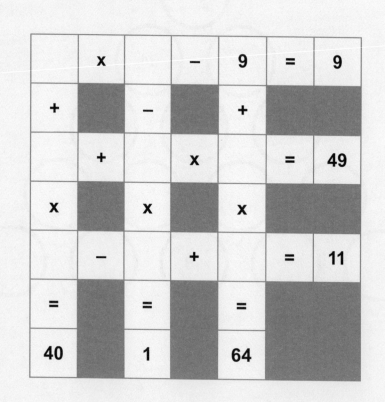

	x		–	9	=	9
+		–		+		
	+		x		=	49
x		x		x		
	–		+		=	11
=		=		=		
40		1		64		

Summing Up

Arrange one of each of the four given numbers, as well as one each of the symbols – (minus), x (times) and + (plus) in every row and column to arrive at the answer at the end of the row or column, making the calculations in the order in which they appear. Some are already in place.

158

2 5 7 9

5	+	7	–	2	x	9	=	90
	▉		▉		▉	–	▉	▉
							=	12
	▉		▉		▉		▉	▉
				7	+		=	54
	▉		▉		▉	x	▉	▉
							=	78
=	▉	=	▉	=	▉	=	▉	▉
34	▉	15	▉	16	▉	14	▉	▉

Total Concentration

The blank squares below should be filled with whole numbers between 1 and 30 inclusive, any of which may occur more than once, or not at all. The numbers in every horizontal row add up to the totals on the right, as do the two long diagonal lines; whilst those in every vertical column add up to the totals along the bottom.

159

							85
17		10		14	3	20	100
	3		15	8	14	19	107
29	16		2		21	4	92
4	11		9		27	13	79
30		5	22	19		26	119
18	23	7		18	12		96
	11	17	6		16		100
119	97	83	79	103	98	114	91

Symbol Sums

Each symbol stands for a different number. In order to reach the correct total at the end of each row and column, what is the value of the circle, pentagon, square and star?

160

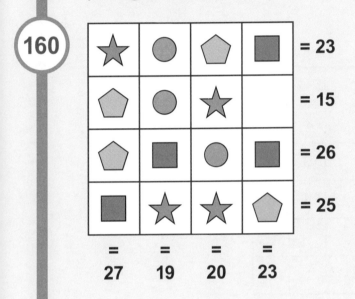

161

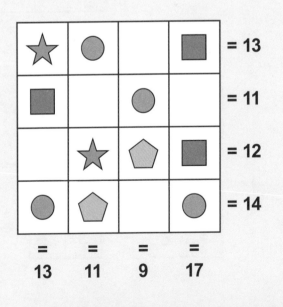

Tile Twister

Place the eight tiles into the puzzle grid so that all adjacent numbers on each tile match up. Tiles may be rotated through 360 degrees, but none may be flipped over.

162

				3	4
				1	3

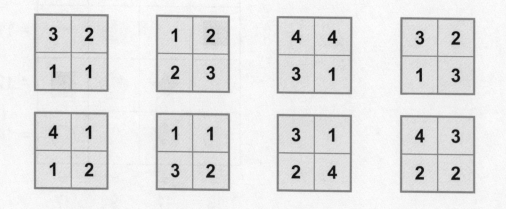

What's the Number?

In the diagram below, what number should replace the question mark?

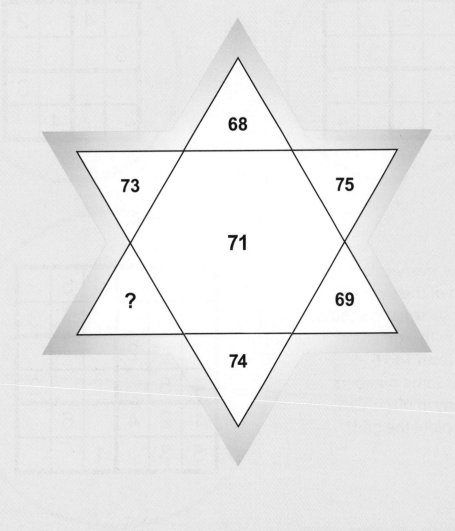

Mini Sudoku

Every row, every column and each of the four smaller boxes of four squares should be filled with a different number from 1 to 4 inclusive. Some numbers are already in place. Can you complete the grid?

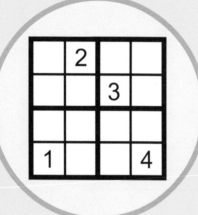

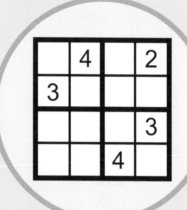

Every row, every column and each of the six smaller boxes of six squares should be filled with a different number from 1 to 6 inclusive. Some numbers are already in place. Can you complete the grid?

Sum Circle

Fill the three empty circles with the symbols +, – and x in some order, to make a sum which totals the number in the middle. Each symbol must be used once and calculations are made in the direction of travel (clockwise).

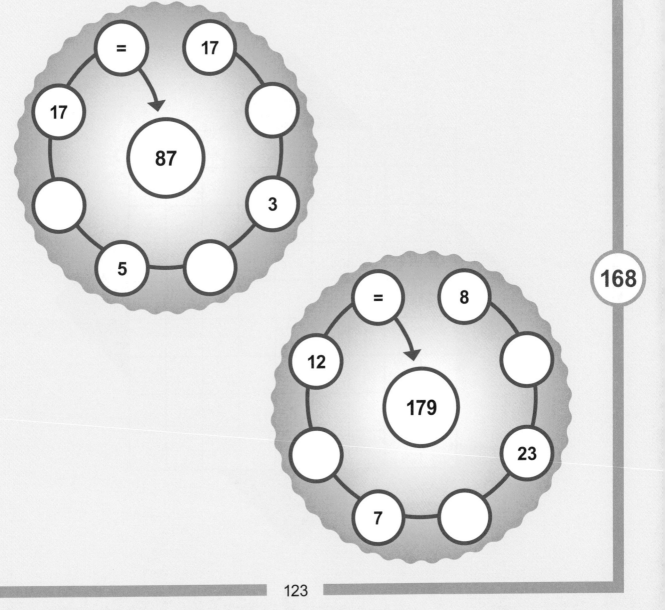

Number Path

Working from one square to another, horizontally or vertically (never diagonally), draw paths to pair up each set of two matching numbers. No path may be shared, and none may enter a square containing a number or part of another path.

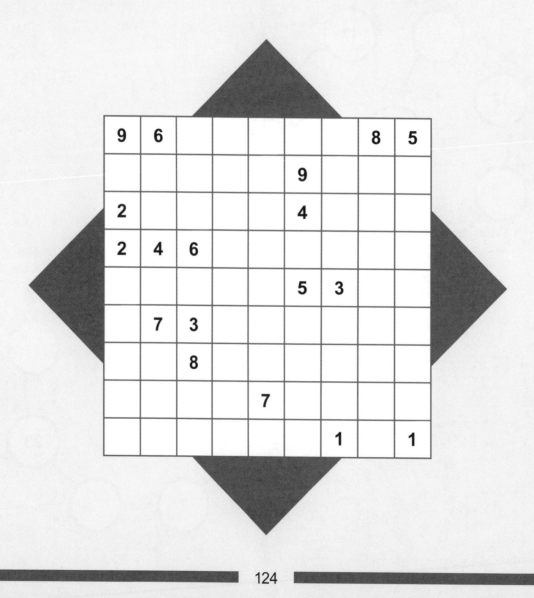

Hexagony

Can you place the hexagons into the grid, so that where any hexagon touches another along a straight line, the number in both triangles is the same? No rotation of any hexagon is allowed!

Number Crunch

Starting at the top left with the number provided, work down from one box to another, applying the mathematical instructions to your running total.

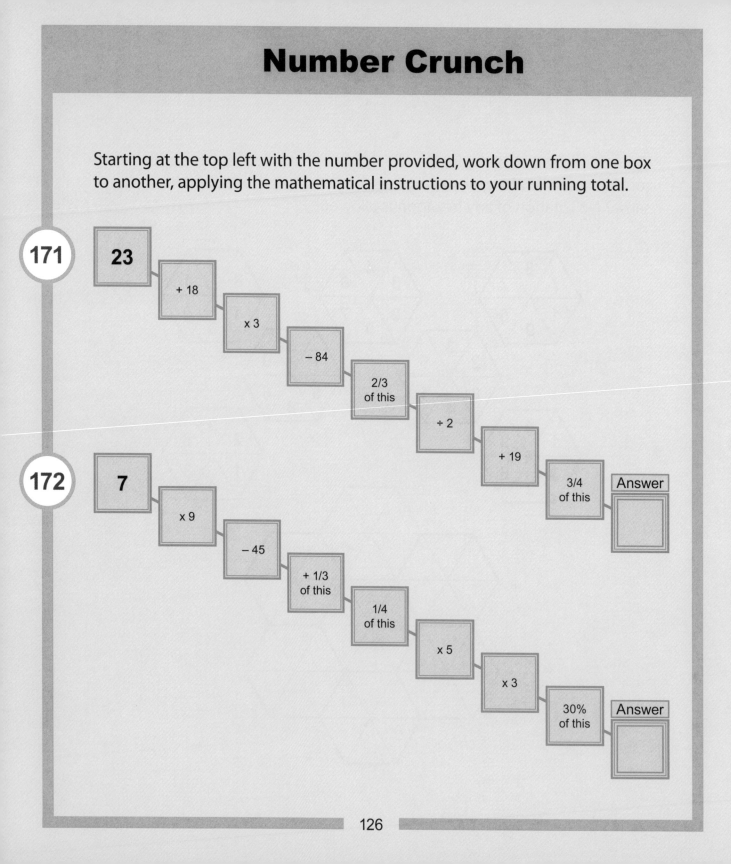

171

23
+ 18
x 3
− 84
2/3 of this
÷ 2
+ 19
3/4 of this
Answer

172

7
x 9
− 45
+ 1/3 of this
1/4 of this
x 5
x 3
30% of this
Answer

Pyramid Plus

The number in each circle is the sum of the two numbers below it. Just work out the missing numbers in every circle!

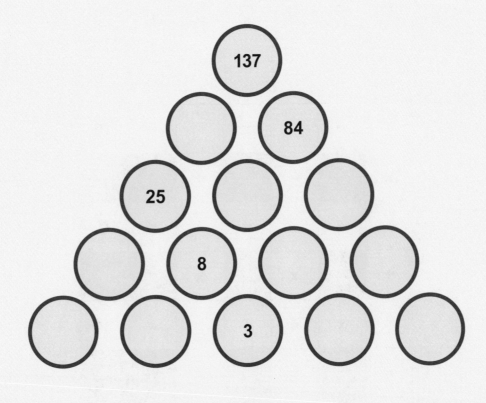

One to Nine

Using the numbers one to nine, complete these six equations (three reading across and three reading downwards). Every number is used once only, and one is already in place.

174

1 2 3 4 5 6 7 8 9

	+		x		=	10
x		−		+		
	−		x		=	9
+		x		x		
	x	4	+		=	34
=		=		=		
26		8		20		

Summing Up

Arrange one of each of the four given numbers, as well as one each of the symbols – (minus), x (times) and + (plus) in every row and column to arrive at the answer at the end of the row or column, making the calculations in the order in which they appear. Some are already in place.

175

3 5 7 8

5	–	3	+	8	x	7	=	70
		x						
							=	30
							=	26
	–		x				=	14
=		=		=		=		
32		18		24		40		

Total Concentration

176

The blank squares below should be filled with whole numbers between 1 and 30 inclusive, any of which may occur more than once, or not at all. The numbers in every horizontal row add up to the totals on the right, as do the two long diagonal lines; whilst those in every vertical column add up to the totals along the bottom.

							105
		13	23	5	21	22	134
24	12	1	6	17	29		100
28	4	27				7	118
19	7		5	10	27		73
29	8	4			26	30	139
	14		9	1	9	11	69
25		3	8			25	110
157	89	74	95	65	155	108	124

Symbol Sums

Each symbol stands for a different number. In order to reach the correct total at the end of each row and column, what is the value of the circle, pentagon, square and star?

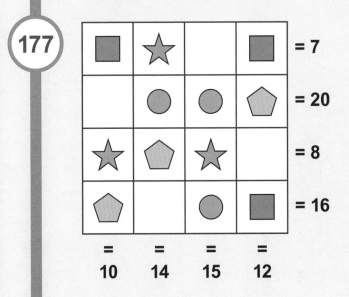

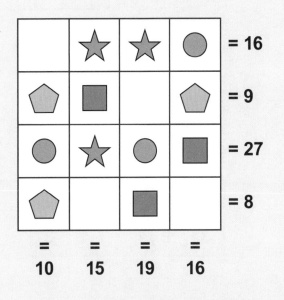

Tile Twister

Place the eight tiles into the puzzle grid so that all adjacent numbers on each tile match up. Tiles may be rotated through 360 degrees, but none may be flipped over.

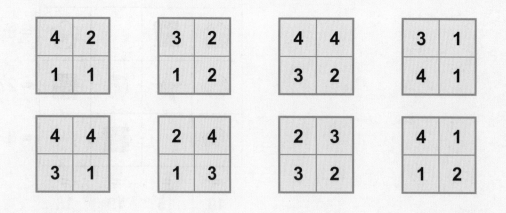

What's the Number?

In the diagram below, what number should replace the question mark?

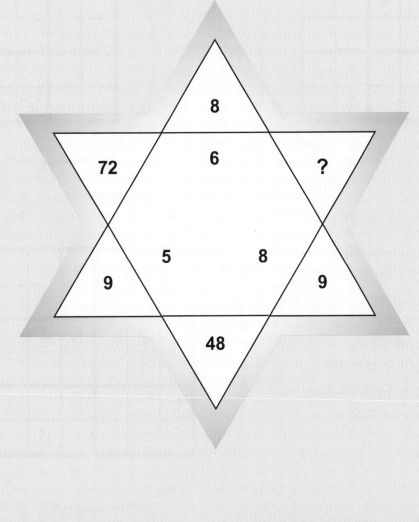

Mini Sudoku

Every row, every column and each of the four smaller boxes of four squares should be filled with a different number from 1 to 4 inclusive. Some numbers are already in place. Can you complete the grid?

181

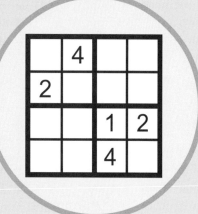

182

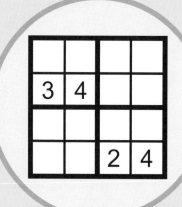

183

Every row, every column and each of the six smaller boxes of six squares should be filled with a different number from 1 to 6 inclusive. Some numbers are already in place. Can you complete the grid?

Sum Circle

Fill the three empty circles with the symbols +, – and x in some order, to make a sum which totals the number in the middle. Each symbol must be used once and calculations are made in the direction of travel (clockwise).

184

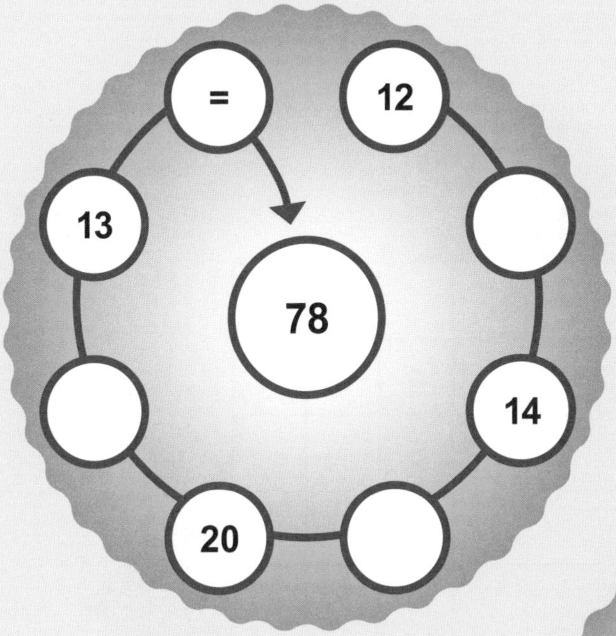

= 12 13 78 14 20

185

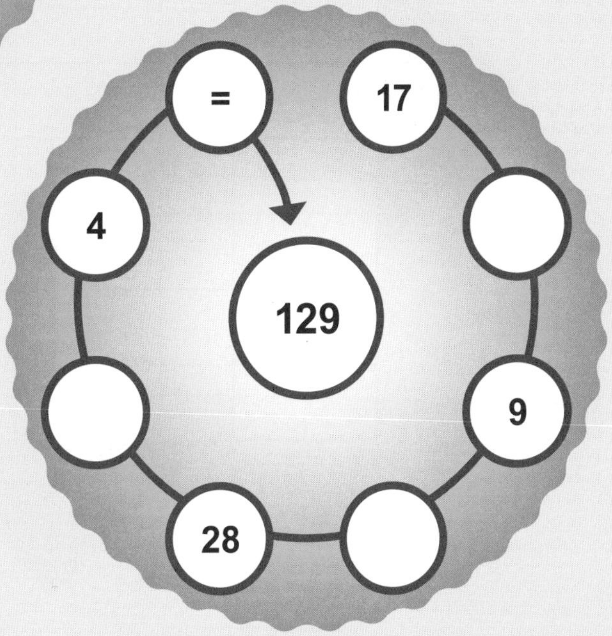

= 17 4 129 9 28

Number Path

Working from one square to another, horizontally or vertically (never diagonally), draw paths to pair up each set of two matching numbers. No path may be shared, and none may enter a square containing a number or part of another path.

186

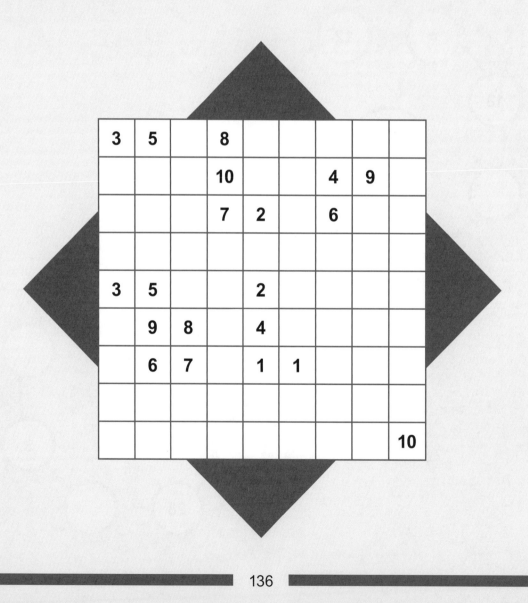

Hexagony

Can you place the hexagons into the grid, so that where any hexagon touches another along a straight line, the number in both triangles is the same? No rotation of any hexagon is allowed!

Number Crunch

Starting at the top left with the number provided, work down from one box to another, applying the mathematical instructions to your running total.

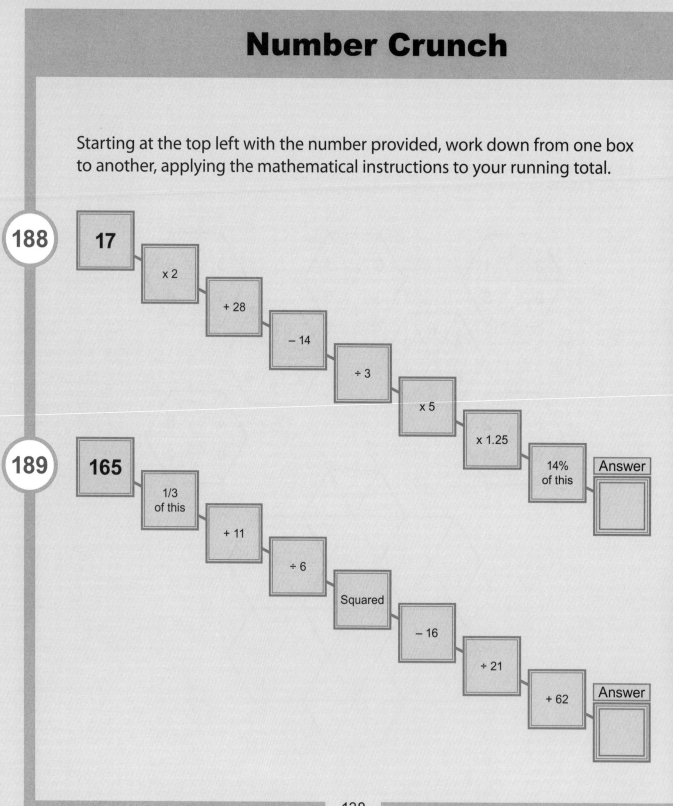

188

17

x 2

+ 28

− 14

÷ 3

x 5

x 1.25

14% of this

Answer

189

165

1/3 of this

+ 11

÷ 6

Squared

− 16

÷ 21

+ 62

Answer

Pyramid Plus

The number in each circle is the sum of the two numbers below it. Just work out the missing numbers in every circle!

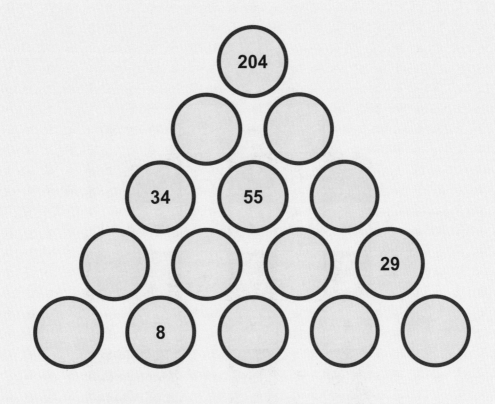

One to Nine

Using the numbers one to nine, complete these six equations (three reading across and three reading downwards). Every number is used once only, and one is already in place.

191

1 2 3 4 5 6 7 8 9

	x		–		=	30
x		+		–		
3	+		x		=	10
+		–		+		
	–		x		=	6
=		=		=		
20		11		7		

Summing Up

Arrange one of each of the four given numbers, as well as one each of the symbols – (minus), x (times) and + (plus) in every row and column to arrive at the answer at the end of the row or column, making the calculations in the order in which they appear. Some are already in place.

1 3 8 9

9	–	3	+	1	x	8	=	56
					+		=	4
							=	98
						x		
	–						=	90
=		=		=		=		
22		20		78		54		

Total Concentration

193

The blank squares below should be filled with whole numbers between 1 and 30 inclusive, any of which may occur more than once, or not at all. The numbers in every horizontal row add up to the totals on the right, as do the two long diagonal lines; whilst those in every vertical column add up to the totals along the bottom.

							147
12	18		22	5		21	115
	28	14	13		30		121
22		4	21	16	13	20	120
29	15			11	20	26	136
29		17	18	26		16	119
	19	19		2	24	28	134
	9	27	25		25		119
127	116	112	156	98	136	119	122

142

Symbol Sums

Each symbol stands for a different number. In order to reach the correct total at the end of each row and column, what is the value of the circle, pentagon, square and star?

194

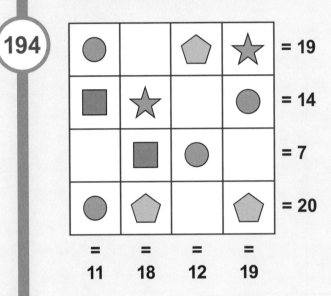

195

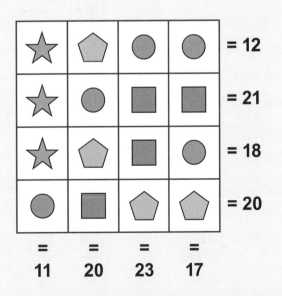

Tile Twister

Place the eight tiles into the puzzle grid so that all adjacent numbers on each tile match up. Tiles may be rotated through 360 degrees, but none may be flipped over.

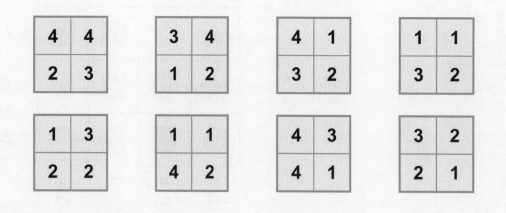

What's the Number?

In the diagram below, what number should replace the question mark?

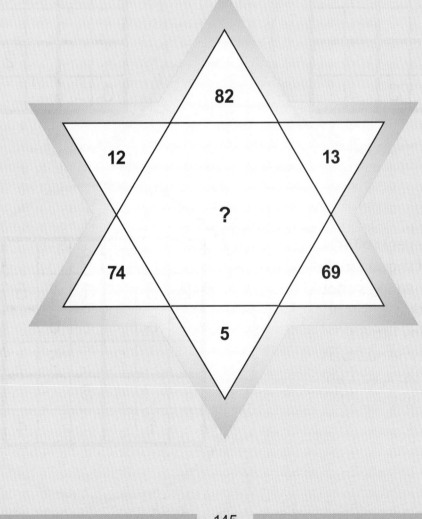

Mini Sudoku

Every row, every column and each of the four smaller boxes of four squares should be filled with a different number from 1 to 4 inclusive. Some numbers are already in place. Can you complete the grid?

198

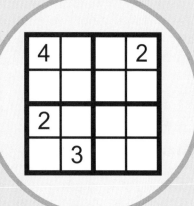

199

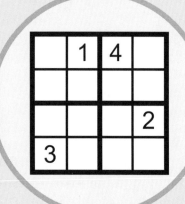

200

Every row, every column and each of the six smaller boxes of six squares should be filled with a different number from 1 to 6 inclusive. Some numbers are already in place. Can you complete the grid?

Sum Circle

Fill the three empty circles with the symbols +, − and x in some order, to make a sum which totals the number in the middle. Each symbol must be used once and calculations are made in the direction of travel (clockwise).

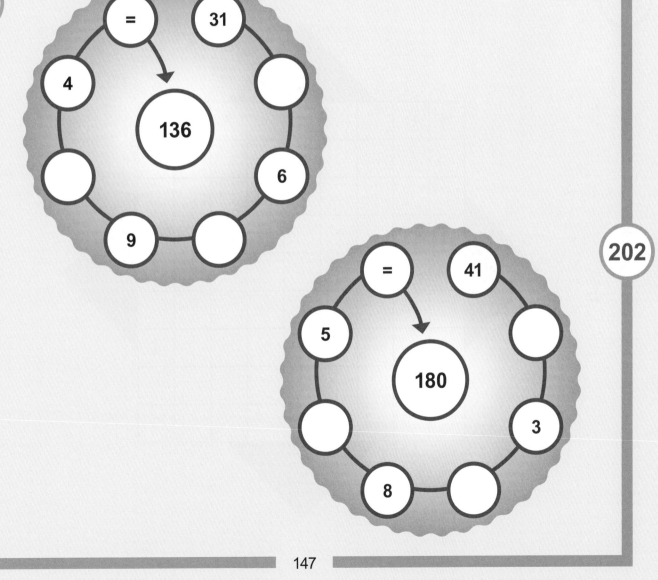

201

202

Number Path

Working from one square to another, horizontally or vertically (never diagonally), draw paths to pair up each set of two matching numbers. No path may be shared, and none may enter a square containing a number or part of another path.

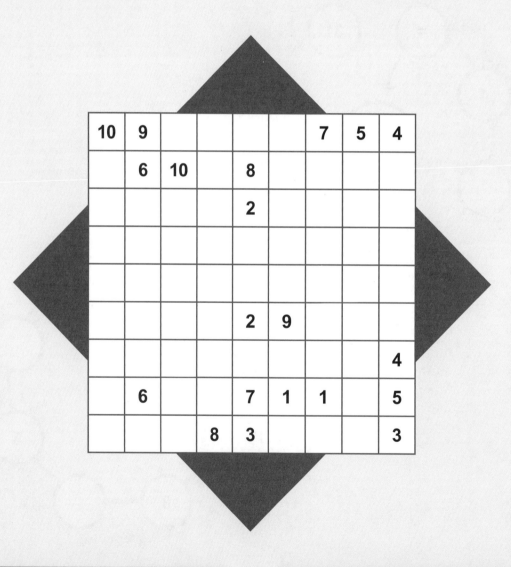

Hexagony

Can you place the hexagons into the grid, so that where any hexagon touches another along a straight line, the number in both triangles is the same? No rotation of any hexagon is allowed!

204

Number Crunch

Starting at the top left with the number provided, work down from one box to another, applying the mathematical instructions to your running total.

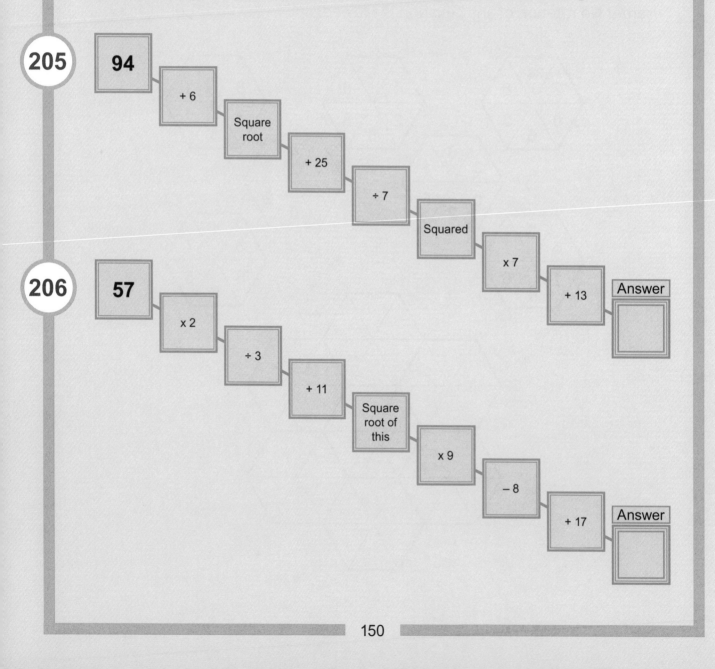

205

94

+ 6

Square root

+ 25

÷ 7

Squared

x 7

+ 13

Answer

206

57

x 2

÷ 3

+ 11

Square root of this

x 9

− 8

+ 17

Answer

Pyramid Plus

The number in each circle is the sum of the two numbers below it. Just work out the missing numbers in every circle!

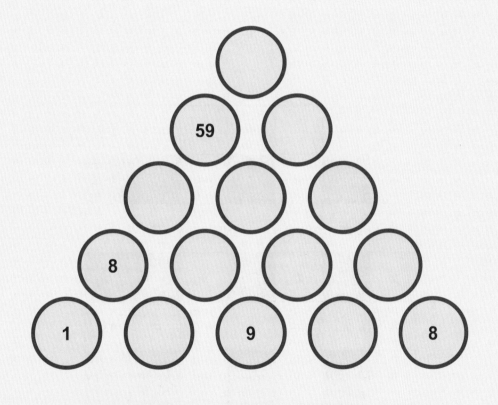

One to Nine

Using the numbers one to nine, complete these six equations (three reading across and three reading downwards). Every number is used once only, and one is already in place.

208

$$1 \quad 2 \quad 3 \quad 4 \quad 5 \quad 6 \quad 7 \quad 8 \quad 9$$

	−		+		=	14
−		+		−		
4	+		−		=	9
x		x		+		
	x		+		=	11
=		=		=		
5		60		9		

Summing Up

Arrange one of each of the four given numbers, as well as one each of the symbols – (minus), x (times) and + (plus) in every row and column to arrive at the answer at the end of the row or column, making the calculations in the order in which they appear. Some are already in place.

2 3 5 7

3	x	7	–	5	+	2	= 18
						=	24
x							
		x			7	=	14
			+				
						=	15
=		=		=		=	
9		28		34		30	

153

Total Concentration

The blank squares below should be filled with whole numbers between 1 and 30 inclusive, any of which may occur more than once, or not at all. The numbers in every horizontal row add up to the totals on the right, as do the two long diagonal lines; whilst those in every vertical column add up to the totals along the bottom.

210

							108

17	16		25		2	11	82
3	3		13	7	20		67
	29	24	19	10		6	101
15		6		11	26		69
30		21	28	13		17	140
8	22	18	14		27	14	108
	19	9		18	5	4	88

108	107	97	110	68	96	69	89

154

Symbol Sums

Each symbol stands for a different number. In order to reach the correct total at the end of each row and column, what is the value of the circle, pentagon, square and star?

211

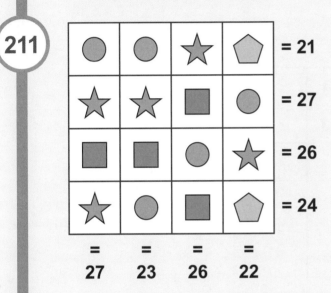

212

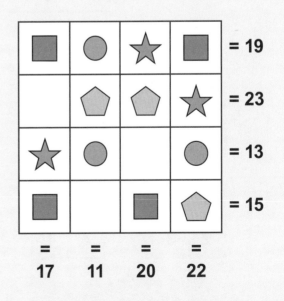

Tile Twister

Place the eight tiles into the puzzle grid so that all adjacent numbers on each tile match up. Tiles may be rotated through 360 degrees, but none may be flipped over.

213

		4	1		
		3	3		

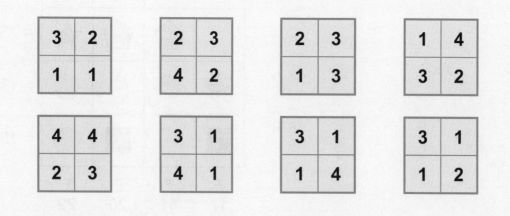

What's the Number?

In the diagram below, what number should replace the question mark?

214

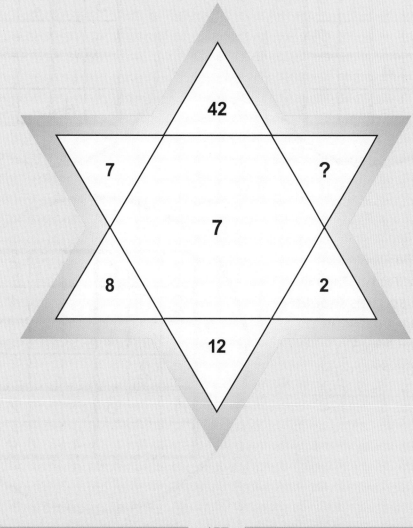

Mini Sudoku

Every row, every column and each of the four smaller boxes of four squares should be filled with a different number from 1 to 4 inclusive. Some numbers are already in place. Can you complete the grid?

215

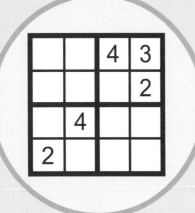

216

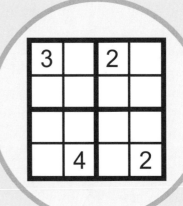

217

Every row, every column and each of the six smaller boxes of six squares should be filled with a different number from 1 to 6 inclusive. Some numbers are already in place. Can you complete the grid?

Sum Circle

Fill the three empty circles with the symbols +, – and x in some order, to make a sum which totals the number in the middle. Each symbol must be used once and calculations are made in the direction of travel (clockwise).

218

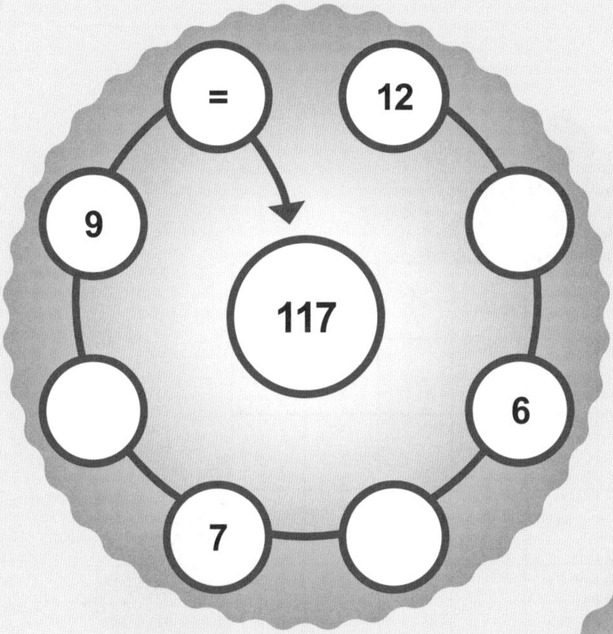

= 12

9

117

6

7

219

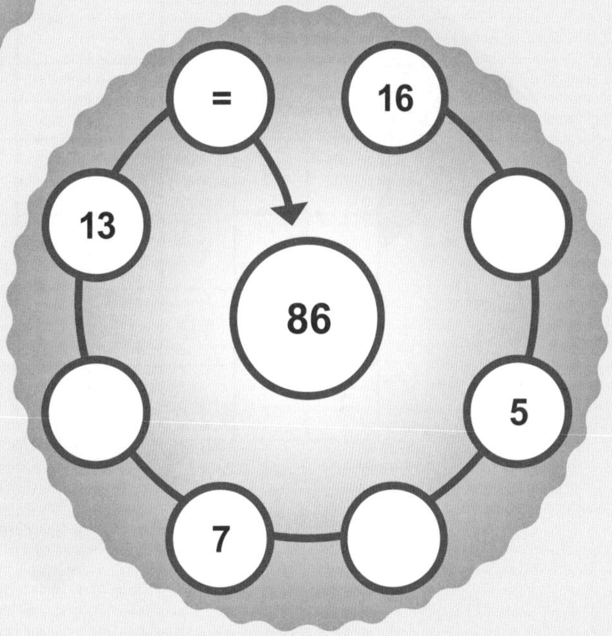

= 16

13

86

5

7

Number Path

Working from one square to another, horizontally or vertically (never diagonally), draw paths to pair up each set of two matching numbers. No path may be shared, and none may enter a square containing a number or part of another path.

220

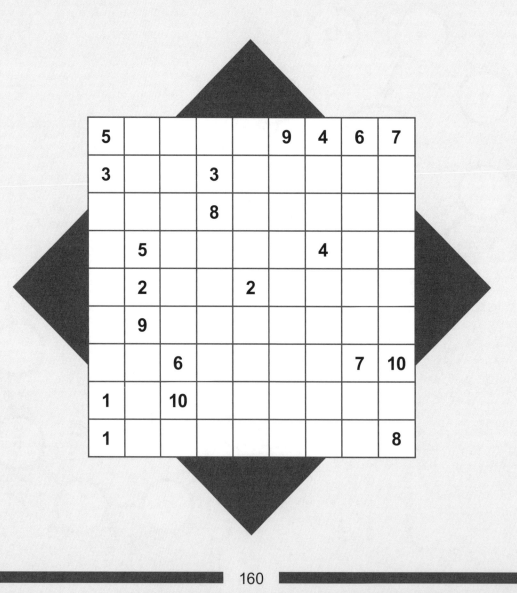

Hexagony

Can you place the hexagons into the grid, so that where any hexagon touches another along a straight line, the number in both triangles is the same? No rotation of any hexagon is allowed!

Number Crunch

Starting at the top left with the number provided, work down from one box to another, applying the mathematical instructions to your running total.

222

| 9 |

Square root of this

x 14

+ 6

÷ 4

Squared

÷ 9

x 3

Answer

223

| 329 |

− 4

÷ 5

x 2

+ 10

÷ 20

− 3

Square root of this

Answer

Pyramid Plus

The number in each circle is the sum of the two numbers below it. Just work out the missing numbers in every circle!

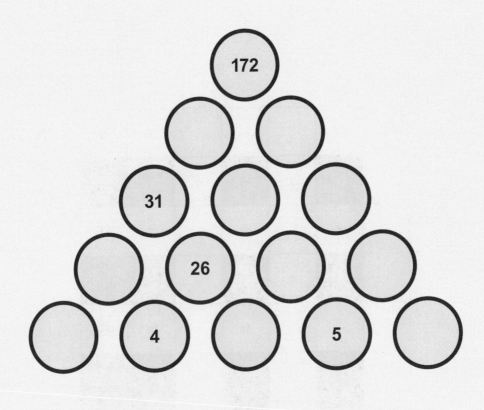

One to Nine

Using the numbers one to nine, complete these six equations (three reading across and three reading downwards). Every number is used once only, and one is already in place.

225

1 2 3 4 5 6 7 8 9

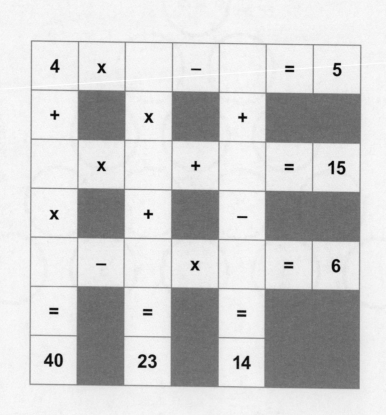

4	x		–		=	5
+		x		+		
	x		+		=	15
x		+		–		
	–		x		=	6
=		=		=		
40		23		14		

Summing Up

Arrange one of each of the four given numbers, as well as one each of the symbols – (minus), x (times) and + (plus) in every row and column to arrive at the answer at the end of the row or column, making the calculations in the order in which they appear. Some are already in place.

226

3 4 7 9

9	–	3	+	4	x	7	=	70
x	■		■		■	–	■	■
							=	96
	■		■		■	x	■	■
							=	64
	■		■		■		■	■
							=	40
=	■	=	■	=	■	=	■	■
32	■	86	■	70	■	25	■	■

Total Concentration

The blank squares below should be filled with whole numbers between 1 and 30 inclusive, any of which may occur more than once, or not at all. The numbers in every horizontal row add up to the totals on the right, as do the two long diagonal lines; whilst those in every vertical column add up to the totals along the bottom.

227

							123
21	27		1	4	6		108
20	9	16		22	5		104
2		8	15	5		8	90
10	2	23	22		1		103
	6	27	13		24	18	137
	25	14	3		11	29	92
20	4			12	24	23	142
104	99	147	109	88	97	132	115

Symbol Sums

Each symbol stands for a different number. In order to reach the correct total at the end of each row and column, what is the value of the circle, pentagon, square and star?

228

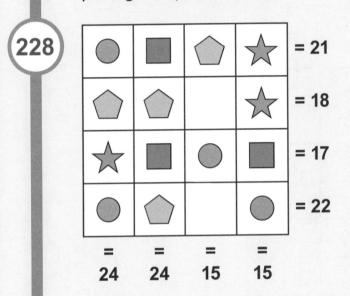

229

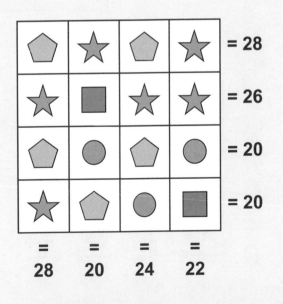

Tile Twister

Place the eight tiles into the puzzle grid so that all adjacent numbers on each tile match up. Tiles may be rotated through 360 degrees, but none may be flipped over.

230

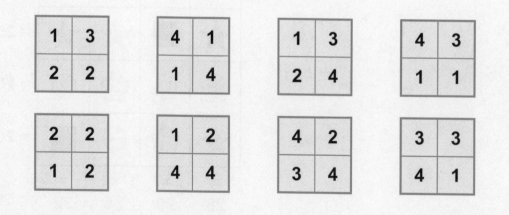

What's the Number?

In the diagram below, what number should replace the question mark?

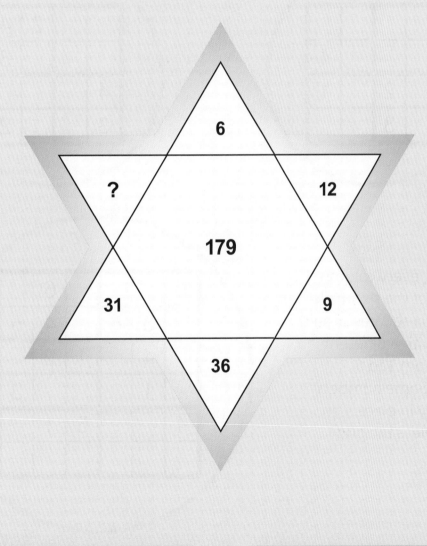

Mini Sudoku

Every row, every column and each of the four smaller boxes of four squares should be filled with a different number from 1 to 4 inclusive. Some numbers are already in place. Can you complete the grid?

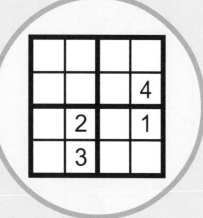

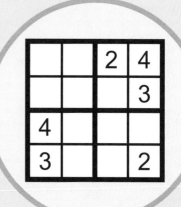

Every row, every column and each of the six smaller boxes of six squares should be filled with a different number from 1 to 6 inclusive. Some numbers are already in place. Can you complete the grid?

Sum Circle

Fill the three empty circles with the symbols +, – and x in some order, to make a sum which totals the number in the middle. Each symbol must be used once and calculations are made in the direction of travel (clockwise).

235

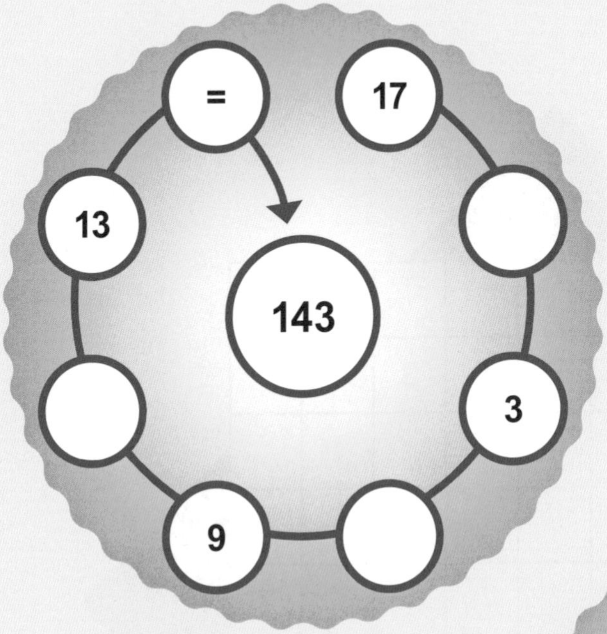

17

=

13

143

3

9

236

=

14

17

100

8

5

171

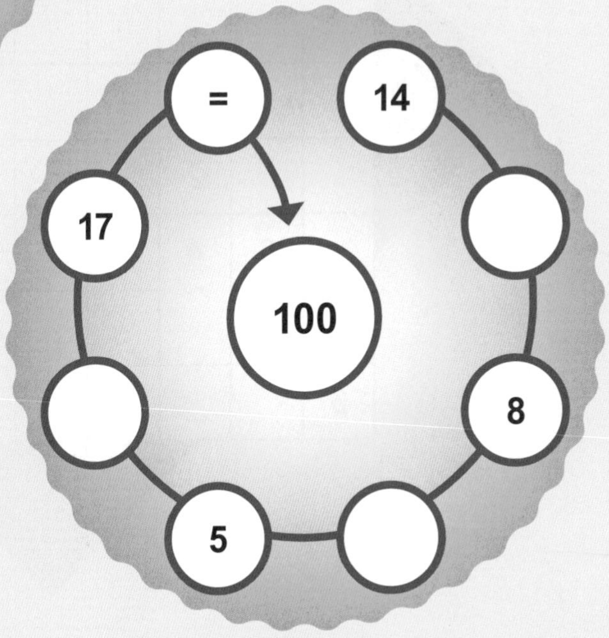

Number Path

Working from one square to another, horizontally or vertically (never diagonally), draw paths to pair up each set of two matching numbers. No path may be shared, and none may enter a square containing a number or part of another path.

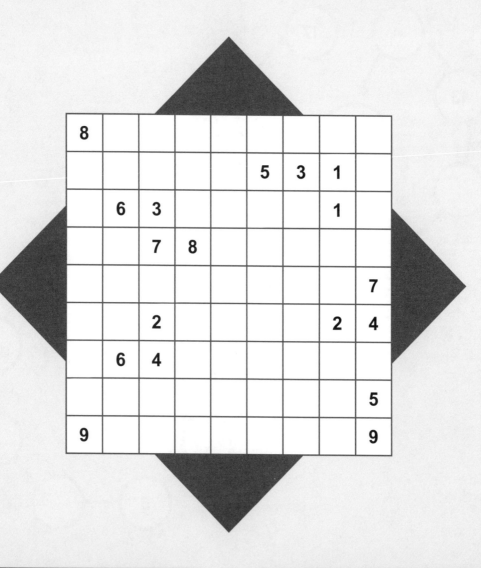

Hexagony

Can you place the hexagons into the grid, so that where any hexagon touches another along a straight line, the number in both triangles is the same? No rotation of any hexagon is allowed!

Number Crunch

Starting at the top left with the number provided, work down from one box to another, applying the mathematical instructions to your running total.

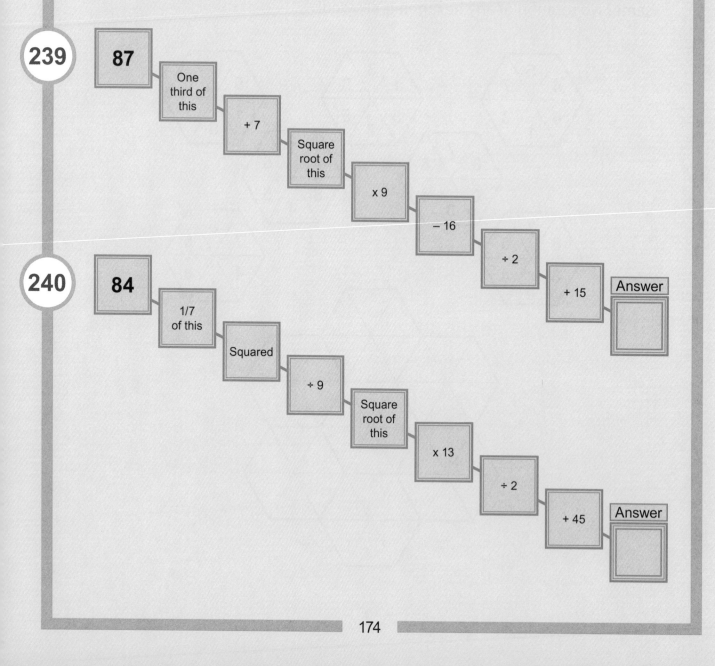

239

87

One third of this

+ 7

Square root of this

x 9

− 16

÷ 2

+ 15

Answer

240

84

1/7 of this

Squared

÷ 9

Square root of this

x 13

÷ 2

+ 45

Answer

Pyramid Plus

The number in each circle is the sum of the two numbers below it. Just work out the missing numbers in every circle!

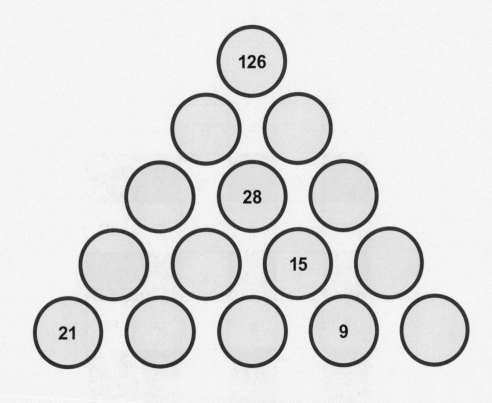

One to Nine

Using the numbers one to nine, complete these six equations (three reading across and three reading downwards). Every number is used once only, and one is already in place.

242

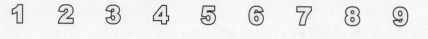

1 2 3 4 5 6 7 8 9

	x		−	9	=	1
+		x		−		
	x		+		=	10
−		+		x		
	+		x		=	80
=		=		=		
3		9		48		

Summing Up

Arrange one of each of the four given numbers, as well as one each of the symbols – (minus), x (times) and + (plus) in every row and column to arrive at the answer at the end of the row or column, making the calculations in the order in which they appear. Some are already in place.

243

3   4   6   9

4	+	3	x	9	–	6	=	57
6	–					=	45
						=	15
						=	25
=		=		=		=	
18		33		60		41	

Total Concentration

The blank squares below should be filled with whole numbers between 1 and 30 inclusive, any of which may occur more than once, or not at all. The numbers in every horizontal row add up to the totals on the right, as do the two long diagonal lines; whilst those in every vertical column add up to the totals along the bottom.

244

							107
	27		19	12	26	19	133
	18	26	5		20	25	116
2		17	27	1	16		89
25	4	24		23		15	125
14	20	18	14	9	6		104
	28			17		8	107
11		11	29		30	15	133
95	131	120	111	88	144	118	100

Symbol Sums

Each symbol stands for a different number. In order to reach the correct total at the end of each row and column, what is the value of the circle, pentagon, square and star?

245

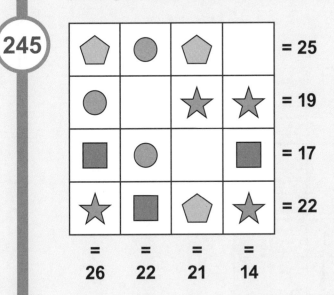

246

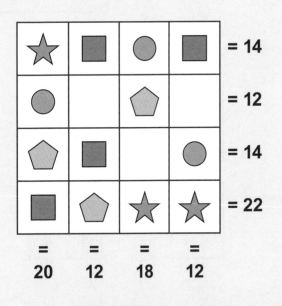

Tile Twister

Place the eight tiles into the puzzle grid so that all adjacent numbers on each tile match up. Tiles may be rotated through 360 degrees, but none may be flipped over.

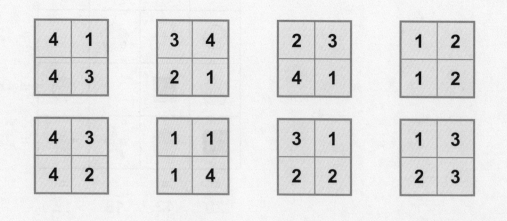

What's the Number?

In the diagram below, what number should replace the question mark?

248

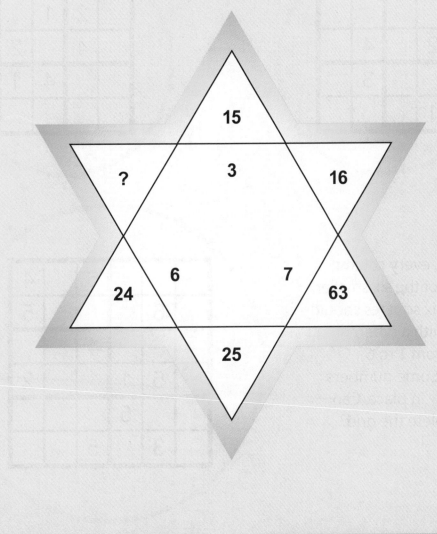

Mini Sudoku

Every row, every column and each of the four smaller boxes of four squares should be filled with a different number from 1 to 4 inclusive. Some numbers are already in place. Can you complete the grid?

249

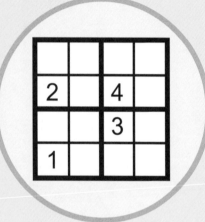

250

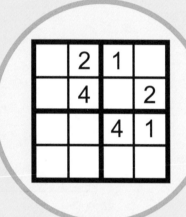

251

Every row, every column and each of the six smaller boxes of six squares should be filled with a different number from 1 to 6 inclusive. Some numbers are already in place. Can you complete the grid?

Sum Circle

Fill the three empty circles with the symbols +, – and x in some order, to make a sum which totals the number in the middle. Each symbol must be used once and calculations are made in the direction of travel (clockwise).

252

253

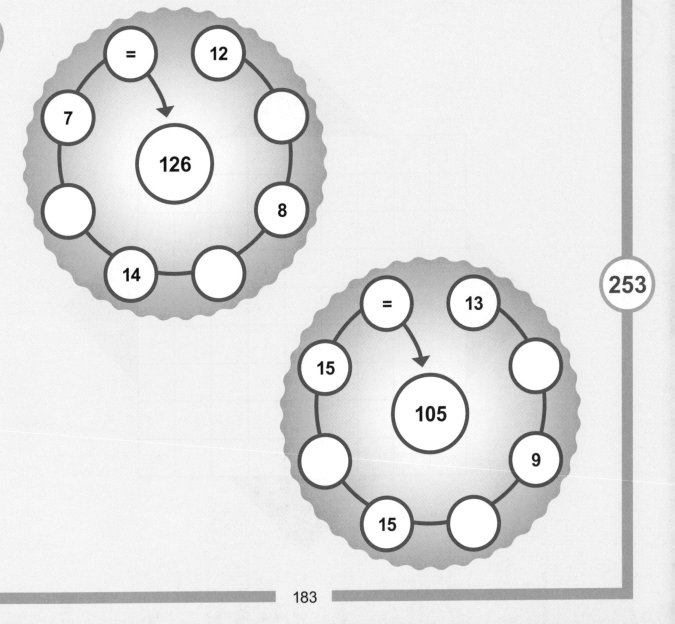

Number Path

Working from one square to another, horizontally or vertically (never diagonally), draw paths to pair up each set of two matching numbers. No path may be shared, and none may enter a square containing a number or part of another path.

254

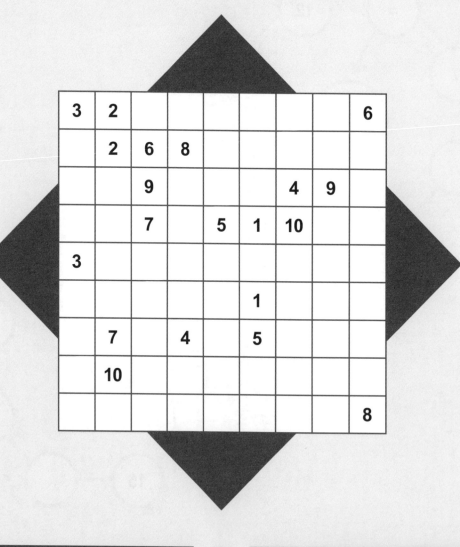

Hexagony

Can you place the hexagons into the grid, so that where any hexagon touches another along a straight line, the number in both triangles is the same? No rotation of any hexagon is allowed!

Number Crunch

Starting at the top left with the number provided, work down from one box to another, applying the mathematical instructions to your running total.

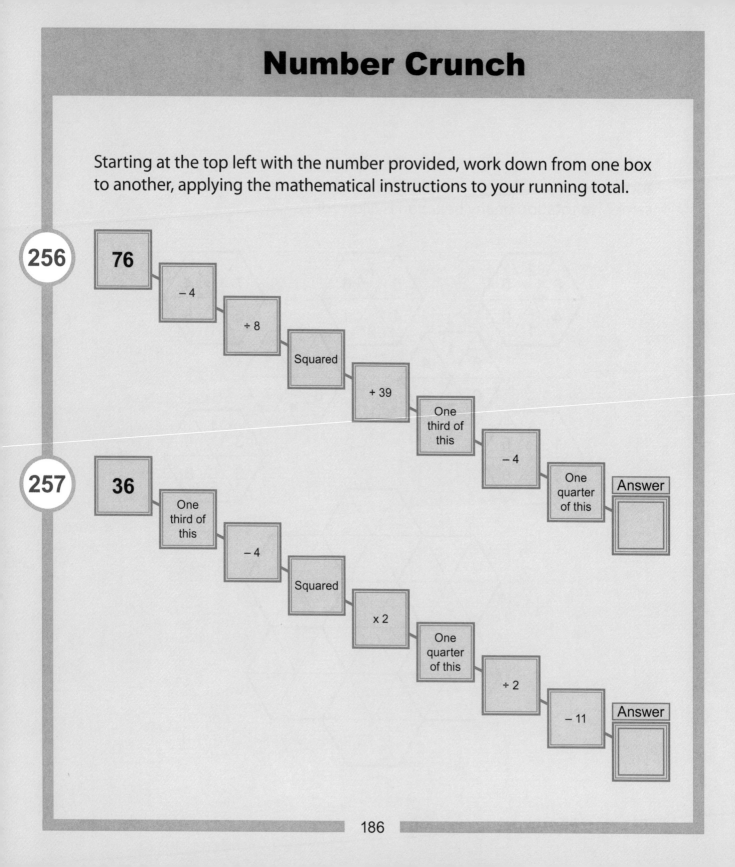

256

76

− 4

÷ 8

Squared

+ 39

One third of this

− 4

One quarter of this

Answer

257

36

One third of this

− 4

Squared

x 2

One quarter of this

÷ 2

− 11

Answer

Pyramid Plus

The number in each circle is the sum of the two numbers below it. Just work out the missing numbers in every circle!

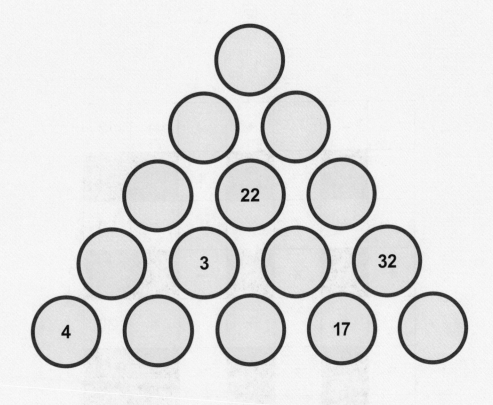

One to Nine

Using the numbers one to nine, complete these six equations (three reading across and three reading downwards). Every number is used once only, and one is already in place.

259

1 2 3 4 5 6 7 8 9

	−		+		=	12
−		+		x		
	+	7	x		=	50
+		x		−		
	x		+		=	20
=		=		=		
8		48		12		

Summing Up

Arrange one of each of the four given numbers, as well as one each of the symbols – (minus), x (times) and + (plus) in every row and column to arrive at the answer at the end of the row or column, making the calculations in the order in which they appear. Some are already in place.

2 3 7 8

7	+	3	x	8	–	2	=	78
							=	12
		–			x		=	64
				3			=	25
=		=		=		=		
23		19		27		33		

Total Concentration

261

The blank squares below should be filled with whole numbers between 1 and 30 inclusive, any of which may occur more than once, or not at all. The numbers in every horizontal row add up to the totals on the right, as do the two long diagonal lines; whilst those in every vertical column add up to the totals along the bottom.

							143
		13	27	1	10	14	96
5	14	23		22		11	115
24	3	2		17	8		81
7		5	13		2	6	66
	8	29	25	11		7	110
16			30	4	10	20	121
	30		9		19	9	99
114	88	88	122	99	89	88	87

Symbol Sums

Each symbol stands for a different number. In order to reach the correct total at the end of each row and column, what is the value of the circle, pentagon, square and star?

262

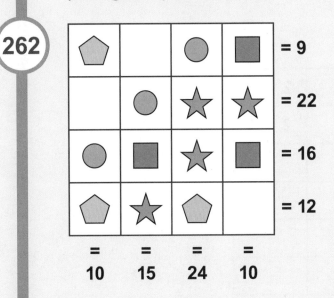

263

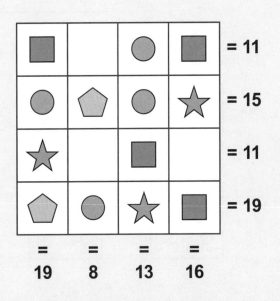

191

Tile Twister

Place the eight tiles into the puzzle grid so that all adjacent numbers on each tile match up. Tiles may be rotated through 360 degrees, but none may be flipped over.

264

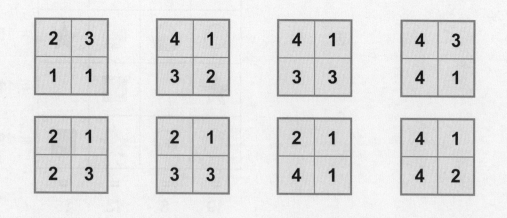

What's the Number?

In the diagram below, what number should replace the question mark?

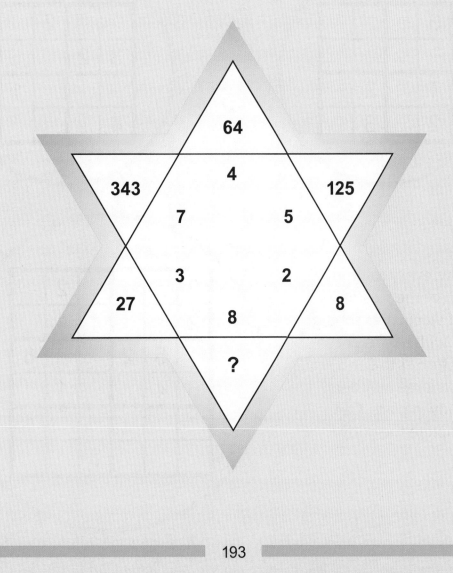

Mini Sudoku

Every row, every column and each of the four smaller boxes of four squares should be filled with a different number from 1 to 4 inclusive. Some numbers are already in place. Can you complete the grid?

266

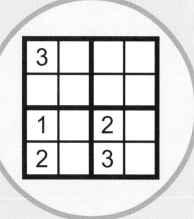

267

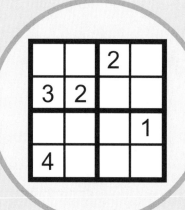

268

Every row, every column and each of the six smaller boxes of six squares should be filled with a different number from 1 to 6 inclusive. Some numbers are already in place. Can you complete the grid?

Sum Circle

Fill the three empty circles with the symbols +, – and x in some order, to make a sum which totals the number in the middle. Each symbol must be used once and calculations are made in the direction of travel (clockwise).

269

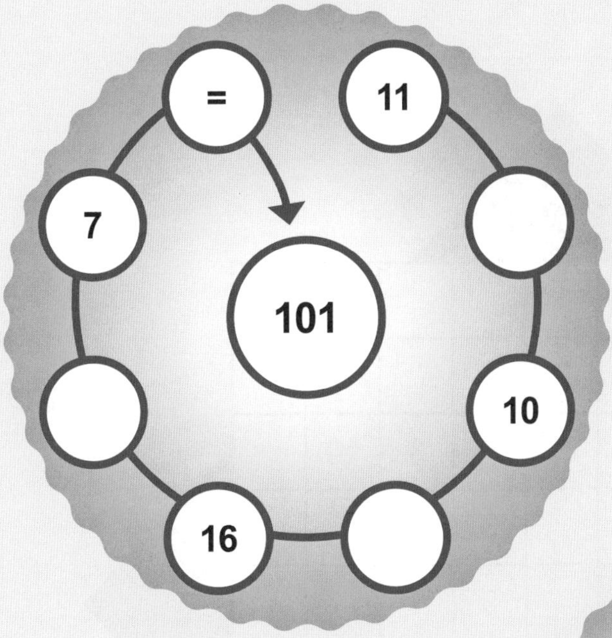

= 11

7

101

10

16

270

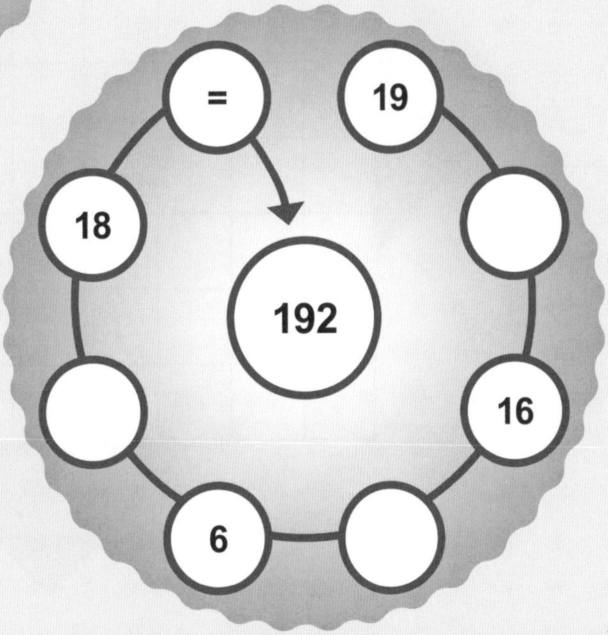

= 19

18

192

16

6

Number Path

Working from one square to another, horizontally or vertically (never diagonally), draw paths to pair up each set of two matching numbers. No path may be shared, and none may enter a square containing a number or part of another path.

271

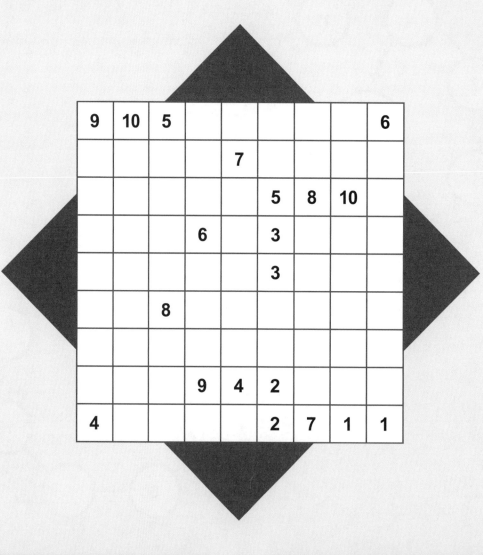

Hexagony

Can you place the hexagons into the grid, so that where any hexagon touches another along a straight line, the number in both triangles is the same? No rotation of any hexagon is allowed!

Number Crunch

Starting at the top left with the number provided, work down from one box to another, applying the mathematical instructions to your running total.

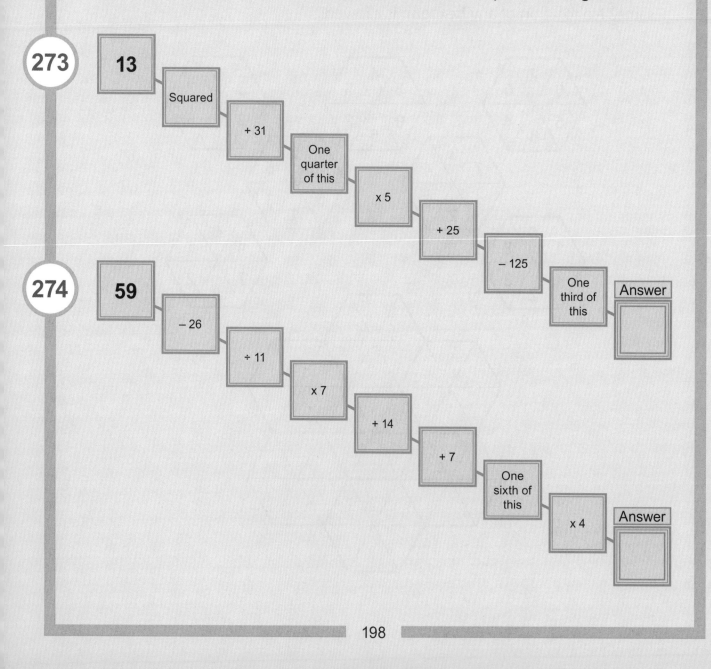

273

13 → Squared → + 31 → One quarter of this → x 5 → + 25 → − 125 → One third of this → Answer

274

59 → − 26 → ÷ 11 → x 7 → + 14 → + 7 → One sixth of this → x 4 → Answer

Pyramid Plus

The number in each circle is the sum of the two numbers below it. Just work out the missing numbers in every circle!

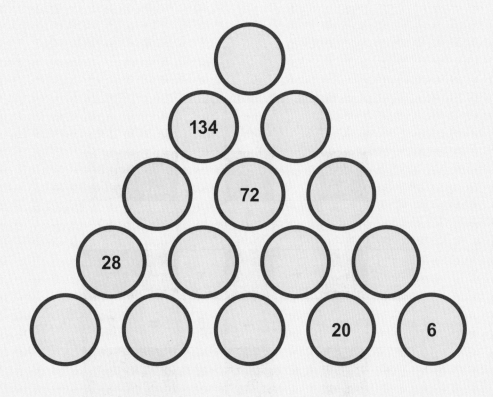

One to Nine

Using the numbers one to nine, complete these six equations (three reading across and three reading downwards). Every number is used once only, and one is already in place.

276

$$1 \quad 2 \quad 3 \quad 4 \quad 5 \quad 6 \quad 7 \quad 8 \quad 9$$

	−		x		=	16
+		x		−		
	+		x		=	12
−		+		x		
	x		−	6	=	21
=		=		=		
8		19		42		

Summing Up

Arrange one of each of the four given numbers, as well as one each of the symbols – (minus), x (times) and + (plus) in every row and column to arrive at the answer at the end of the row or column, making the calculations in the order in which they appear. Some are already in place.

1 4 6 9

4	+	6	–	1	x	9	=	81
	■		■	6	■		=	11
							=	19
9							=	34
=		=		=		=	■	■
27		57		59		36		

Total Concentration

The blank squares below should be filled with whole numbers between 1 and 30 inclusive, any of which may occur more than once, or not at all. The numbers in every horizontal row add up to the totals on the right, as do the two long diagonal lines; whilst those in every vertical column add up to the totals along the bottom.

278

							87
	5	4	5	18	28		120
21	21	23			4	24	137
27	6	17		3		9	110
	26	20	3	24	10		101
14		25	19	11		1	112
29	2		19		8	23	123
		1	18	28	27		114
143	98	102	119	129	116	110	97

Symbol Sums

Each symbol stands for a different number. In order to reach the correct total at the end of each row and column, what is the value of the circle, cross, pentagon, square and star?

279

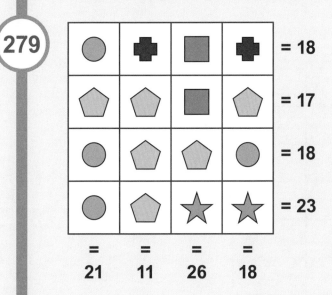

280

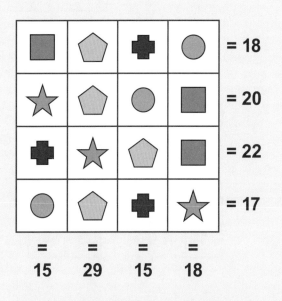

Tile Twister

Place the eight tiles into the puzzle grid so that all adjacent numbers on each tile match up. Tiles may be rotated through 360 degrees, but none may be flipped over.

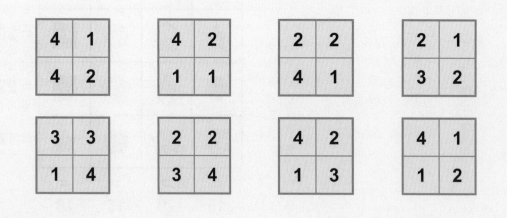

What's the Number?

In the diagram below, what number should replace the question mark?

282

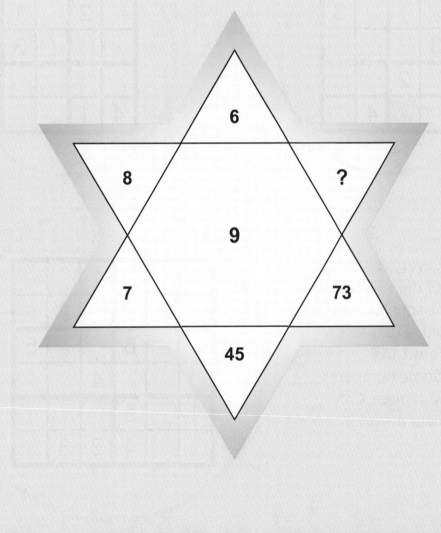

Mini Sudoku

Every row, every column and each of the four smaller boxes of four squares should be filled with a different number from 1 to 4 inclusive. Some numbers are already in place. Can you complete the grid?

283

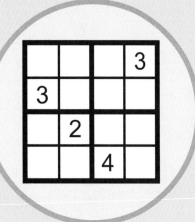

284

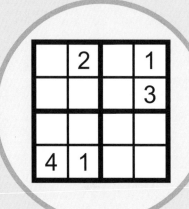

285

Every row, every column and each of the six smaller boxes of six squares should be filled with a different number from 1 to 6 inclusive. Some numbers are already in place. Can you complete the grid?

Sum Circle

Fill the three empty circles with the symbols +, – and x in some order, to make a sum which totals the number in the middle. Each symbol must be used once and calculations are made in the direction of travel (clockwise).

286

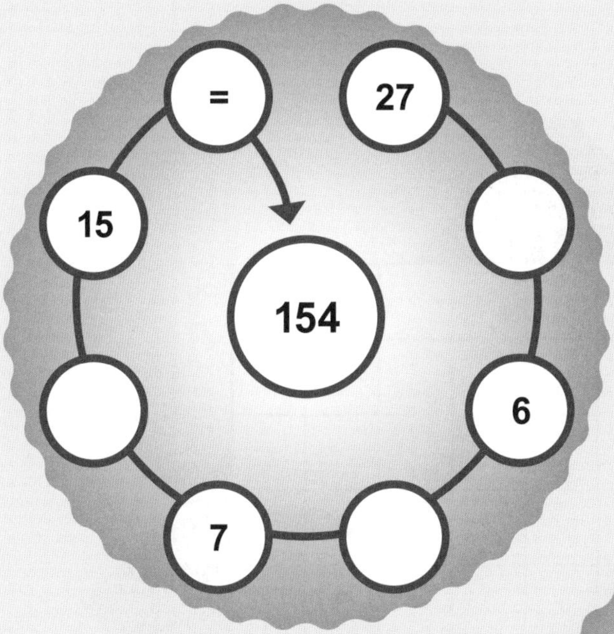

=   27

15

154

6

7

287

=   18

39

86

7

5

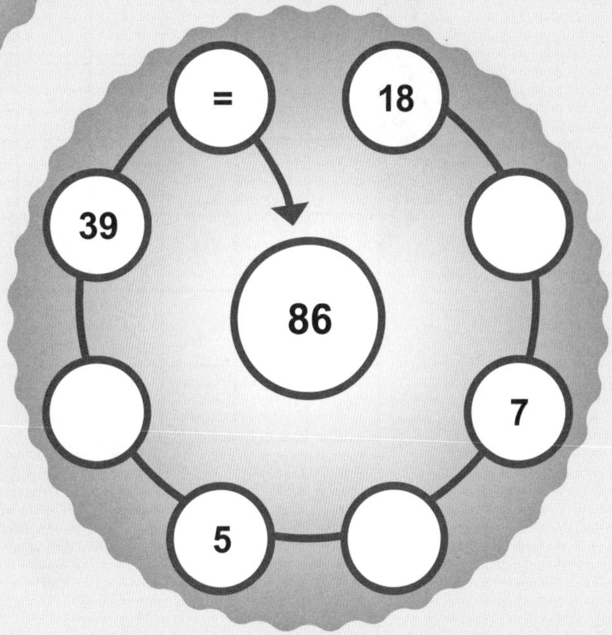

Number Path

Working from one square to another, horizontally or vertically (never diagonally), draw paths to pair up each set of two matching numbers. No path may be shared, and none may enter a square containing a number or part of another path.

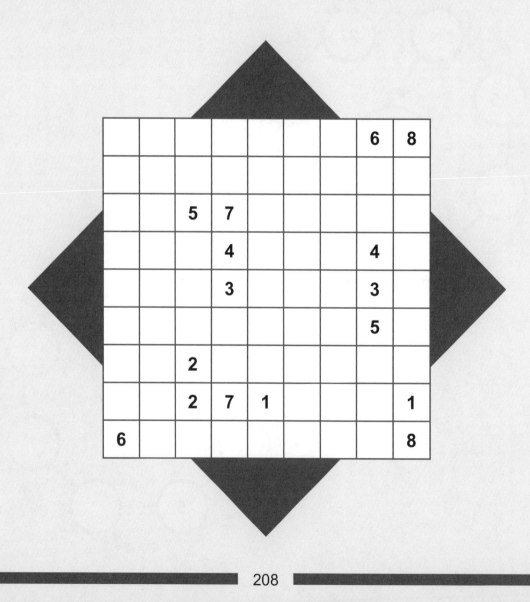

Hexagony

Can you place the hexagons into the grid, so that where any hexagon touches another along a straight line, the number in both triangles is the same? No rotation of any hexagon is allowed!

Number Crunch

Starting at the top left with the number provided, work down from one box to another, applying the mathematical instructions to your running total.

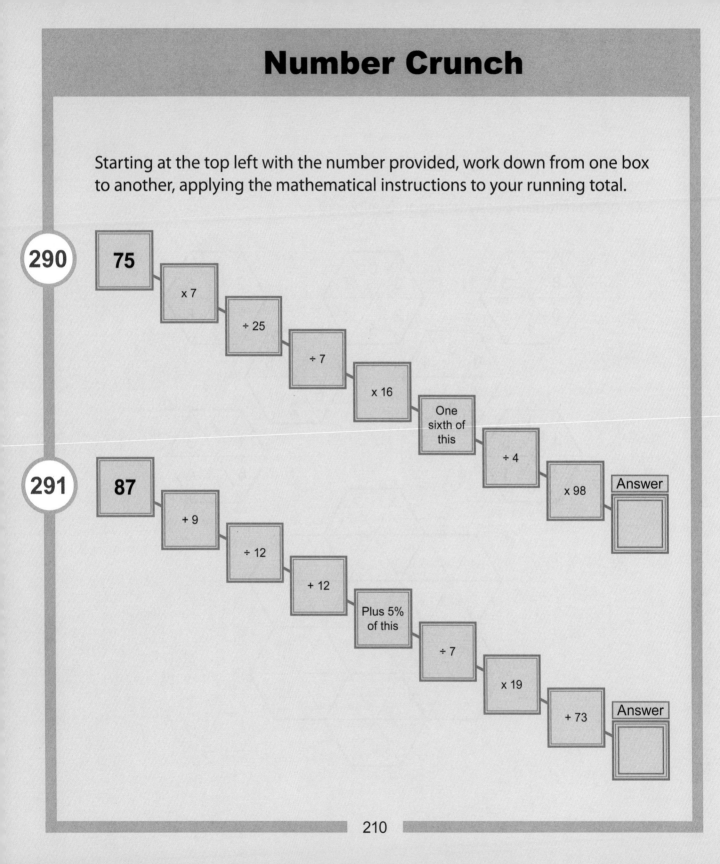

290

75 → x 7 → ÷ 25 → ÷ 7 → x 16 → One sixth of this → ÷ 4 → x 98 → Answer

291

87 → + 9 → ÷ 12 → + 12 → Plus 5% of this → ÷ 7 → x 19 → + 73 → Answer

Pyramid Plus

The number in each circle is the sum of the two numbers below it. Just work out the missing numbers in every circle!

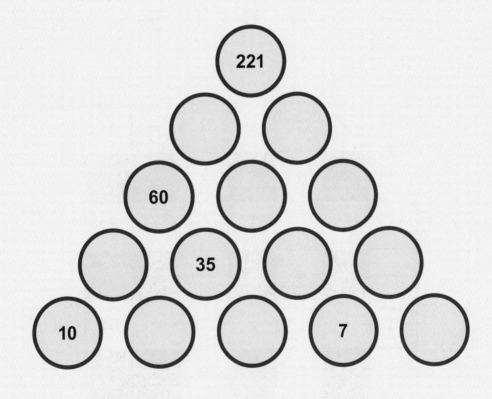

One to Nine

Using the numbers one to nine, complete these six equations (three reading across and three reading downwards). Every number is used once only, and one is already in place.

1 2 3 4 5 6 7 8 9

	x	7	+		=	11
+		+		x		
	x		−		=	42
−		x		+		
	+		x		=	64
=		=		=		
4		96		20		

Summing Up

Arrange one of each of the four given numbers, as well as one each of the symbols – (minus), x (times) and + (plus) in every row and column to arrive at the answer at the end of the row or column, making the calculations in the order in which they appear. Some are already in place.

294

3 5 7 8

3	+	8	–	7	x	5	=	20
	■		■		■		■	■
							=	40
	■	x	■		■		■	■
				5			=	42
	■		■		■		■	■
							=	16
=	■	=	■	=	■	=	■	■
14	■	8	■	54	■	57	■	■

Total Concentration

The blank squares below should be filled with whole numbers between 1 and 30 inclusive, any of which may occur more than once, or not at all. The numbers in every horizontal row add up to the totals on the right, as do the two long diagonal lines; whilst those in every vertical column add up to the totals along the bottom.

295

							75
6		13		18	19	7	95
	23		17	24		9	121
20	12			14		19	101
11	16	23	17		8		104
24	3	9	20	7	25		109
22	10			18	22	14	130
10		11	2	15		1	90
121	112	101	102	109	118	87	80

Symbol Sums

Each symbol stands for a different number. In order to reach the correct total at the end of each row and column, what is the value of the circle, cross, pentagon, square and star?

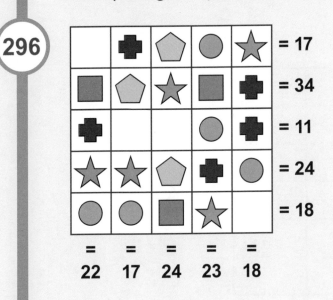

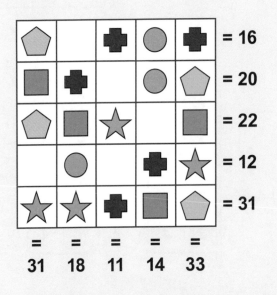

Tile Twister

298

Place the eight tiles into the puzzle grid so that all adjacent numbers on each tile match up. Tiles may be rotated through 360 degrees, but none may be flipped over.

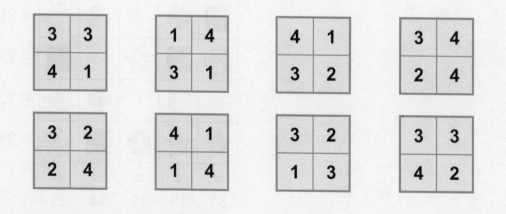

What's the Number?

In the diagram below, what number should replace the question mark?

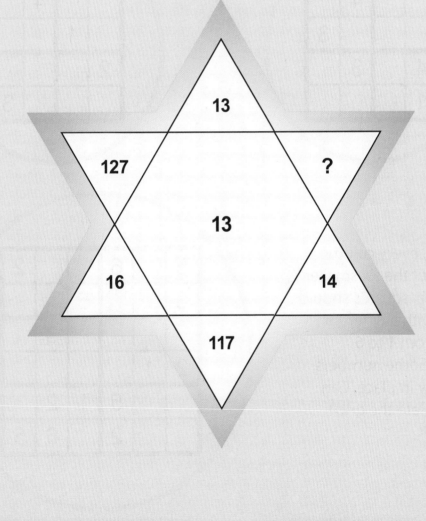

Mini Sudoku

Every row, every column and each of the four smaller boxes of four squares should be filled with a different number from 1 to 4 inclusive. Some numbers are already in place. Can you complete the grid?

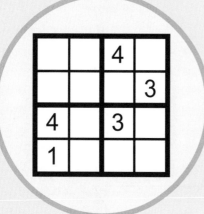

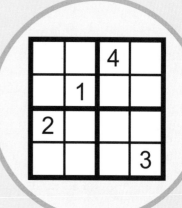

Every row, every column and each of the six smaller boxes of six squares should be filled with a different number from 1 to 6 inclusive. Some numbers are already in place. Can you complete the grid?

Sum Circle

Fill the three empty circles with the symbols +, – and x in some order, to make a sum which totals the number in the middle. Each symbol must be used once and calculations are made in the direction of travel (clockwise).

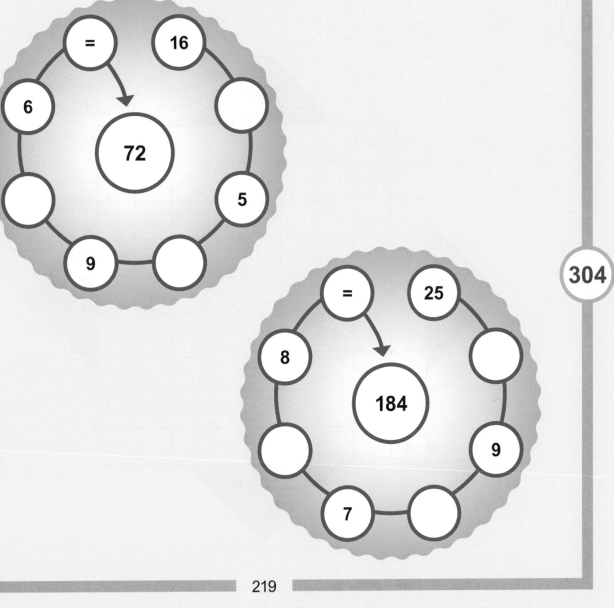

Number Path

Working from one square to another, horizontally or vertically (never diagonally), draw paths to pair up each set of two matching numbers. No path may be shared, and none may enter a square containing a number or part of another path.

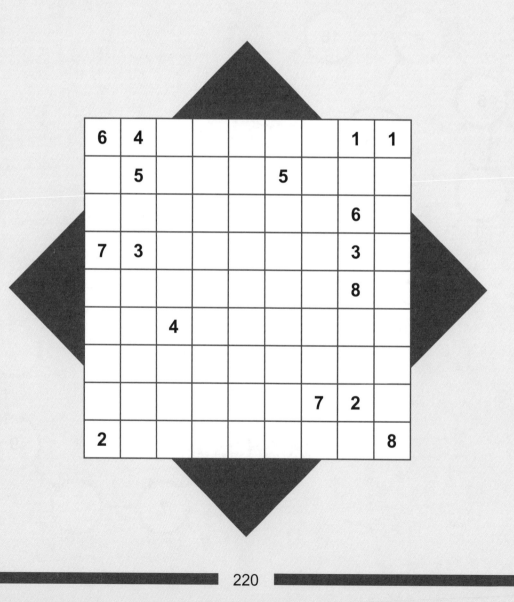

1

94 – 16 = 78, 78 ÷ 2 = 39, 39 ÷ 3 x 2 = 26, 26 + 14 = 40, 40 ÷ 5 x 3 = 24, 24 x 3 = 72, 72 + 28 = 100

2

47 – 38 = 9, 9^2 = 81, 81 ÷ 3 = 27, 27 + 9 = 36, square root of 36 = 6, 6 x 7 = 42, 42 – 18 = 24

3

105
56 49
30 26 23
14 16 10 13
4 10 6 4 9

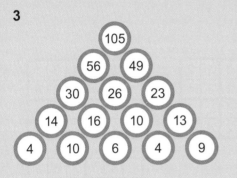

4

4	x	6	–	9	=	15
+		x		+		
8	–	1	x	3	=	21
–		+		x		
2	x	5	+	7	=	17
=		=		=		
10		11		84		

5

3	+	8	x	2	–	7	=	15
–		–		+		+		
2	+	7	–	3	x	8	=	48
+		+		x		x		
7	–	3	+	8	x	2	=	24
x		x		–		–		
8	x	2	–	7	+	3	=	12
=		=		=		=		
64		8		33		27		

6

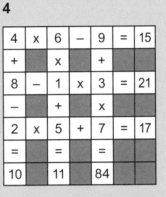

							119
22	30	1	18	23	6	21	121
24	12	20	27	16	24	15	138
7	17	22	11	3	20	30	110
23	4	29	17	28	9	22	132
25	1	16	2	29	28	26	127
8	26	14	18	25	10	27	128
12	13	19	11	5	19	21	100
121	103	121	104	129	116	162	133

7

Circle = 3, Pentagon = 5, Square = 2, Star = 8.

8

Circle = 7, Pentagon = 3, Square = 1, Star = 6.

9

4	4	4	2	2	4
3	2	2	1	1	3
3	2	2	1	1	3
2	3	3	2	2	1
2	3	3	2	2	1
2	3	3	4	4	3

10

79 – The numbers on opposite points of the star total the number in the middle.

11

2	3	4	1
1	4	3	2
3	1	2	4
4	2	1	3

12

4	3	1	2
2	1	3	4
1	4	2	3
3	2	4	1

13

2	5	6	4	3	1
1	3	4	5	2	6
6	2	5	3	1	4
4	1	3	6	5	2
3	6	2	1	4	5
5	4	1	2	6	3

14

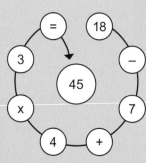

15

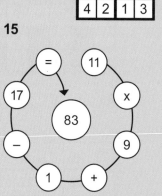

16

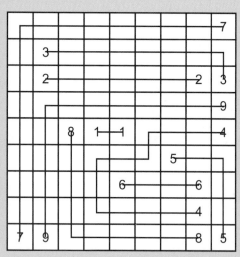

17

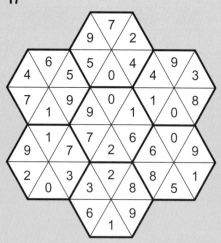

18

6 ÷ 3 = 2, 2² = 4, 4 x 8 = 32, 32 ÷ 8 x 3 = 12, 12 + 98 = 110, 10% of 110 = 11, 11 x 12 = 132

19

51 ÷ 3 = 17, 17 + 18 = 35, 35 ÷ 5 x 4 = 28, 28 ÷ 4 x 3 = 21, 21 + 37 = 58, 58 − 49 = 9, 9 x 8 = 72

20

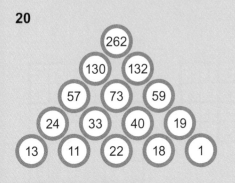

21

8	−	1	x	5	=	35
+		+		x		
2	x	9	+	3	=	21
−		x		+		
4	x	6	−	7	=	17
=		=		=		
6		60		22		

22

5	+	9	x	3	−	6	=	36
−		x		x		+		
3	x	5	−	6	+	9	=	18
x		−		+		x		
9	+	6	x	5	−	3	=	72
+		+				−		
6	−	3	x	9	+	5	=	32
=		=		=		=		
24		42		14		40		

23

							138
18	18	3	24	2	6	22	93
2	3	17	11	6	15	11	65
12	23	19	10	13	5	29	111
12	9	10	30	19	25	14	119
7	26	17	13	1	8	4	76
4	14	1	5	16	15	8	63
27	20	16	7	9	21	28	128
82	113	83	100	66	95	116	114

24

Circle = 4, Pentagon = 7, Square = 2, Star = 8.

25

Circle = 5, Pentagon = 6, Square = 3, Star = 9.

26

4	3	3	3	3	1
4	2	2	3	3	4
4	2	2	3	3	4
2	1	1	4	4	1
2	1	1	4	4	1
1	1	1	2	2	2

27

9 – The numbers in the outer points of the star total the number in the middle.

28

3	2	1	4
4	1	2	3
1	3	4	2
2	4	3	1

29

3	2	1	4
1	4	3	2
2	1	4	3
4	3	2	1

30

5	4	2	6	3	1
6	3	1	2	5	4
1	2	5	4	6	3
3	6	4	1	2	5
4	5	6	3	1	2
2	1	3	5	4	6

31

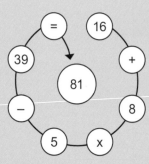

32

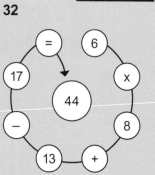

33

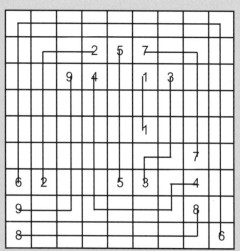

34

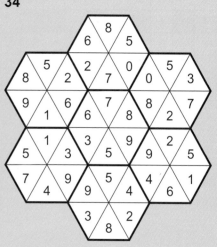

35

10 ÷ 5 x 2 = 4, 4² = 16, 16 ÷ 4 x 3 = 12, 12 x 9 = 108, 108 ÷ 6 = 18, 18 + 48 = 66, 66 ÷ 3 = 22

36

56 + 15 = 71, 71 − 7 = 64, 64 ÷ 4 = 16, square root of 16 = 4, 4 + 69 = 73, 73 − 14 = 59, 59 + 23 = 82

37

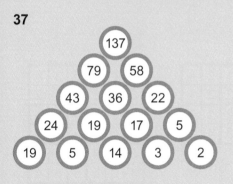

38

2	+	7	−	5	=	4
+		−		x		
6	x	3	−	8	=	10
x		+		−		
9	−	1	x	4	=	32
=		=		=		
72		5		36		

39

6	x	9	−	4	+	7	=	57
−		+		x		−		
4	+	7	−	9	x	6	=	12
x		−		−		x		
7	−	4	x	6	+	9	=	27
+		x		+		+		
9	+	6	−	7	x	4	=	32
=		=		=		=		
23		72		37		13		

40

							81
20	2	28	6	22	24	1	103
5	14	1	30	7	10	21	88
6	29	23	17	21	27	13	136
11	4	23	20	5	3	9	75
22	24	12	28	16	26	4	132
25	2	8	7	30	25	18	115
15	27	29	26	8	3	19	127
104	102	124	134	109	118	85	137

41

Circle = 6, Pentagon = 3, Square = 2, Star = 1.

42

Circle = 1, Pentagon = 8, Square = 9, Star = 6.

Solutions

43

3	3	3	1	1	1
2	1	1	2	2	4
2	1	1	2	2	4
4	3	3	2	2	3
4	3	3	2	2	3
3	4	4	1	1	1

44

3 – The numbers on opposite points of the star are multiplied to reach the number in the middle.

45

1	3	2	4
4	2	1	3
3	1	4	2
2	4	3	1

46

3	1	2	4
4	2	3	1
2	4	1	3
1	3	4	2

47

2	4	1	6	3	5
3	5	6	1	4	2
6	3	2	4	5	1
4	1	5	3	2	6
5	6	4	2	1	3
1	2	3	5	6	4

48
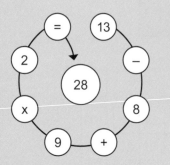

49
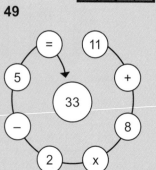

50
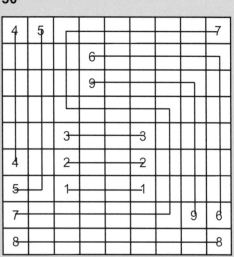

51
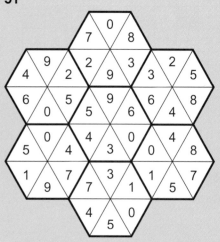

226

52

90 ÷ 5 = 18, 18 ÷ 3 x 2 = 12, 12 ÷ 4 x 3 = 9, 9 x 8 = 72, 72 + 28 = 100, 100 + 20 = 120, 120 ÷ 3 = 40

53

1001 x 5 = 5005, 5005 − 355 = 4650, 10% of 4650 = 465, 465 ÷ 5 = 93, 93 ÷ 3 = 31, 31 + 29 = 60, 60 ÷ 4 = 15

54

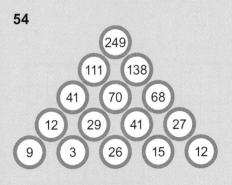

55

5	+	4	x	7	=	63
−		x		+		
3	x	9	−	1	=	26
x		+		x		
2	x	6	+	8	=	20
=		=		=		
4		42		64		

56

2	+	8	x	5	−	4	=	46
x		−		−		+		
5	x	4	−	2	+	8	=	26
−		+		x		x		
4	+	2	x	8	−	5	=	43
+		x		+		−		
8	x	5	+	4	−	2	=	42
=		=		=		=		
14		30		28		58		

57

							94
9	27	25	10	17	17	13	118
11	3	24	16	22	10	23	109
18	12	30	16	19	26	23	144
14	24	5	11	2	26	29	111
4	15	15	27	9	13	18	101
28	12	1	20	6	21	25	113
14	19	21	8	20	22	7	111
98	112	121	108	95	135	138	90

58

Circle = 3, Pentagon = 2, Square = 6, Star = 7.

59

Circle = 5, Pentagon = 9, Square = 4, Star = 8.

Solutions

60

1	2	2	1	1	2
3	4	4	2	2	2
3	4	4	2	2	2
4	2	2	3	3	3
4	2	2	3	3	3
1	2	2	1	1	4

61

5 – Each single digit number in the outer point of the star is multiplied by the central number to reach the total in the opposite point of the star.

62

1	4	3	2
2	3	4	1
3	2	1	4
4	1	2	3

63

1	2	4	3
3	4	2	1
2	1	3	4
4	3	1	2

64

5	4	1	2	6	3
6	2	3	5	4	1
2	3	5	4	1	6
4	1	6	3	2	5
1	5	2	6	3	4
3	6	4	1	5	2

65

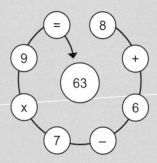

66

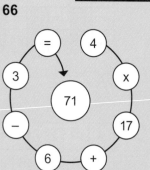

67

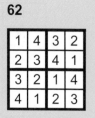

68

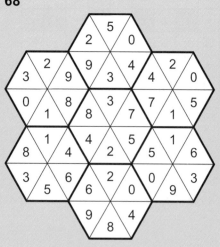

228

69

31 − 15 = 16, 16 + 4 = 20, 20 + 18 = 38, 38 ÷ 2 = 19, 19 − 11 = 8, 8^2 = 64, 64 + 146 = 210

70

60% of 200 = 120, 120 ÷ 4 = 30, 30 + 10 = 40, 40 x 4 = 160, 160 ÷ 20 = 8, 8 x 11 = 88, 88 − 42 = 46

71

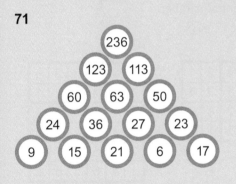

72

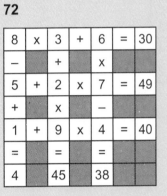

8	x	3	+	6	=	30
−		+		x		
5	+	2	x	7	=	49
+		x		−		
1	+	9	x	4	=	40
=		=		=		
4		45		38		

73

3	+	7	−	9	x	6	=	6
x		−		+		x		
9	−	3	x	6	+	7	=	43
+		x		−		−		
6	x	9	+	7	−	3	=	58
−		+		x		+		
7	−	6	+	3	x	9	=	36
=		=		=		=		
26		42		24		48		

74

							47
11	6	2	15	29	10	5	78
30	21	9	4	24	1	12	101
4	12	23	20	11	8	25	103
22	28	10	3	1	13	7	84
7	16	19	14	17	26	3	102
30	2	13	9	28	5	16	103
6	8	28	18	15	14	27	116
110	93	104	83	125	77	95	107

75

Circle = 3, Pentagon = 4, Square = 5, Star = 9.

76

Circle = 1, Pentagon = 7, Square = 8, Star = 6.

Solutions

77

2	3	3	3	3	2
1	3	3	1	1	3
1	3	3	1	1	3
1	1	1	4	4	4
1	1	1	4	4	4
4	2	2	3	3	2

78

16 – Working clockwise from the top, the numbers represent the running total of numbers in the preceding two points of the star, ending with the central number.

79

3	2	4	1
4	1	2	3
2	3	1	4
1	4	3	2

80

3	4	2	1
2	1	3	4
1	2	4	3
4	3	1	2

81

4	2	1	5	3	6
6	5	3	4	2	1
5	6	2	1	4	3
3	1	4	2	6	5
2	3	5	6	1	4
1	4	6	3	5	2

82

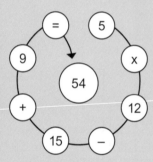

83

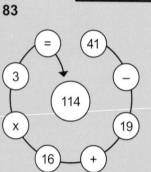

84

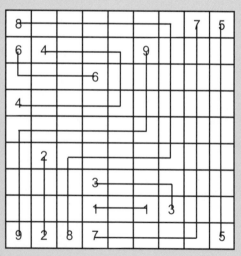

85

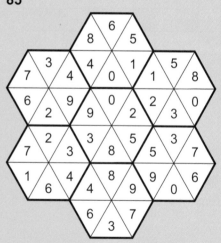

230

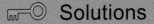

86

95 + 18 = 113, 113 − 72 = 41, 41 x 2 = 82, 82 x 1.5 = 123, 123 − 16 = 107, 107 − 17 = 90, 90 x 4 = 360

87

2^2 = 4, 4 x 9 = 36, square root of 36 = 6, 6 x 7 = 42, 42 ÷ 3 = 14, 14 + 8 = 22, 22 + 38 = 60

88

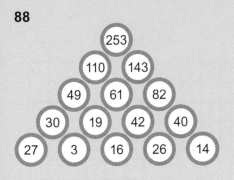

89

4	+	2	x	5	=	30
+		x		−		
6	+	9	−	3	=	12
−		+		x		
8	−	1	x	7	=	49
=		=		=		
2		19		14		

90

6	+	4	x	8	−	3	=	77
−		+		−		x		
3	x	8	−	4	+	6	=	26
x		x		x		+		
4	−	3	x	6	+	8	=	14
+		−		+		−		
8	+	6	−	3	x	4	=	44
=		=		=		=		
20		30		27		22		

91

5	17	27	6	14	25	26	120
7	15	24	18	25	5	13	107
21	4	3	12	23	4	26	93
11	21	22	1	16	19	20	110
28	20	17	3	27	24	8	127
2	2	10	29	30	23	30	126
28	18	29	9	22	19	1	126
102	97	132	78	157	119	124	75

102

92

Circle = 9, Pentagon = 3, Square = 7, Star = 4.

93

Circle = 2, Pentagon = 8, Square = 1, Star = 6.

Solutions

94

4	3	3	1	1	4
4	2	2	2	2	4
4	2	2	2	2	4
3	3	3	4	4	1
3	3	3	4	4	1
1	2	2	3	3	4

95

250 – In each of the opposite points of the star, the two-digit number is multiplied by the central number to reach the three-digit number.

96

2	3	1	4
1	4	2	3
4	2	3	1
3	1	4	2

97

3	1	2	4
2	4	1	3
4	2	3	1
1	3	4	2

98

4	2	3	5	6	1
6	5	1	3	2	4
3	6	4	2	1	5
5	1	2	6	4	3
2	4	5	1	3	6
1	3	6	4	5	2

99

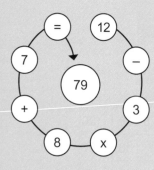

100

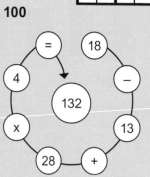

101

102

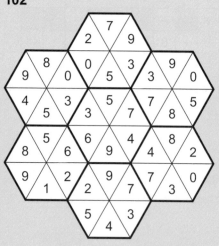

103

35 ÷ 5 = 7, 7 + 27 = 34, 34 x 2 = 68, 68 ÷ 4 = 17, 17 − 8 = 9, square root of 9 = 3, 3 x 15 = 45

104

67 − 22 = 45, 45 ÷ 9 = 5, 5^2 = 25, 25 x 5 = 125, 125 + 25 = 150, 10% of 150 = 15, 15 + 29 = 44

105

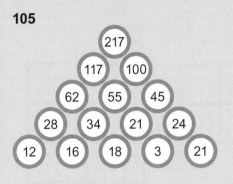

106

8	−	6	x	4	=	8
+		x		+		
1	+	3	x	9	=	36
x		+		x		
5	x	7	−	2	=	33
=		=		=		
45		25		26		

107

5	+	9	x	2	−	7	=	21
−		−		+		+		
2	x	5	−	7	+	9	=	12
+		x		x		x		
7	−	2	x	9	+	5	=	50
x		+		−		−		
9	+	7	−	5	x	2	=	22
=		=		=		=		
90		15		76		78		

108

6	19	26	5	18	20	16	110
25	6	7	14	15	9	21	97
18	27	8	19	4	17	13	106
7	24	12	8	22	14	3	90
28	9	20	23	2	17	12	111
21	23	29	10	13	11	1	108
30	15	22	10	16	11	24	128
135	123	124	89	90	99	90	65

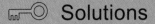

109

Circle = 7, Pentagon = 9, Square = 5, Star = 3.

110

Circle = 4, Pentagon = 8, Square = 3, Star = 5.

Solutions

111

4	1	1	3	3	1
2	4	4	4	4	3
2	4	4	4	4	3
1	4	4	2	2	2
1	4	4	2	2	2
3	3	3	1	1	3

112

32 – Starting at the top and working clockwise,
7 – 4 = 3 x 4 = 12 – 4 = 8 x 4 = 32 x 4 = 128.

113

3	4	2	1
1	2	4	3
4	3	1	2
2	1	3	4

114

3	4	1	2
2	1	4	3
4	2	3	1
1	3	2	4

115

4	6	2	5	3	1
3	1	5	2	4	6
5	2	4	1	6	3
6	3	1	4	5	2
2	4	3	6	1	5
1	5	6	3	2	4

116

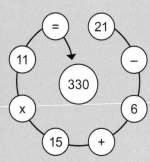

117

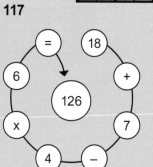

118

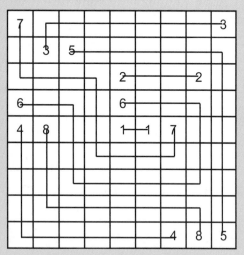

119

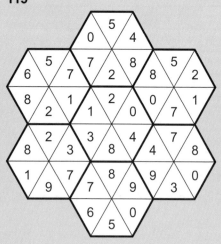

234

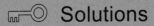

120

9 + 14 = 23, 23 x 2 = 46, 46 − 19 = 27, 27 ÷ 3 x 2 = 18, 18 ÷ 9 = 2, 2 + 1 = 3, 3 x 7 = 21

121

12^2 = 144, 144 ÷ 3 = 48, 48 ÷ 6 = 8, 8 x 5 = 40, 40 x 1.5 = 60, 60 ÷ 5 = 12, 12 x 11 = 132

122

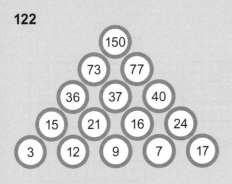

123

9	−	3	x	8	=	48
+		x		−		
2	+	6	x	5	=	40
x		−		x		
7	+	4	−	1	=	10
=		=		=		
77		14		3		

124

4	+	7	x	3	−	8	=	25
x		−		+		−		
8	−	3	x	7	+	4	=	39
−		x		x		+		
3	x	4	−	8	+	7	=	11
+		+		−		x		
7	x	8	+	4	−	3	=	57
=		=		=		=		
36		24		76		33		

125

13	3	10	18	12	26	30	112
3	29	2	9	19	4	16	82
27	11	25	1	17	8	22	111
20	6	21	11	29	5	15	107
12	28	2	28	14	23	10	117
7	4	13	5	24	9	6	68
1	8	7	27	30	26	25	124
83	89	80	99	145	101	124	126

69

126

Circle = 8, Pentagon = 1, Square = 2, Star = 6.

127

Circle = 4, Pentagon = 8, Square = 5, Star = 3.

128

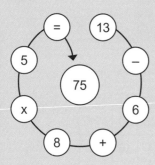

1	2	2	4	4	2
2	1	1	3	3	2
2	1	1	3	3	2
3	2	2	3	3	4
3	2	2	3	3	4
4	4	4	1	1	3

129

16 – The star is made of two overlapping triangles, and the three numbers in the points of each triangle total the central number.

130

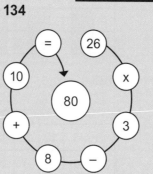

4	3	2	1
1	2	4	3
3	4	1	2
2	1	3	4

131

2	3	4	1
1	4	3	2
3	2	1	4
4	1	2	3

132

3	1	5	4	2	6
2	6	4	5	3	1
5	3	2	6	1	4
6	4	1	2	5	3
1	5	6	3	4	2
4	2	3	1	6	5

133

= 13 5 − 75 6 x 8 +

134

= 26 10 x 80 3 + 8 −

135

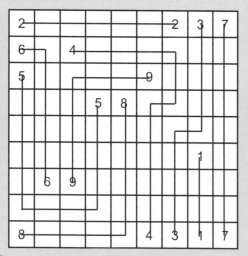

136

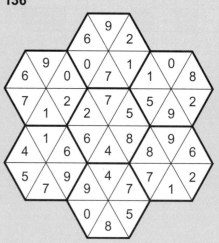

137

85 ÷ 5 = 17, 17 x 2 = 34, 34 + 8 = 42, 42 x 2 = 84,
84 ÷ 7 = 12, 12 + 88 = 100, 24% of 100 = 24

138

2006 − 1008 = 998, 998 ÷ 2 = 499, 499 − 9 = 490,
490 ÷ 70 = 7, 7 x 3 = 21, 21 + 8 = 29, 29 x 2 = 58

139

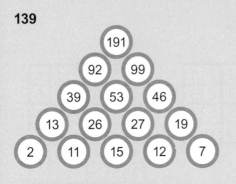

140

4	+	1	x	7	=	35
x		+		−		
6	+	8	−	2	=	12
−		x		+		
3	x	5	+	9	=	24
=		=		=		
21		45		14		

141

5	x	8	+	2	−	6	=	36
+		−		x		+		
6	−	2	x	5	+	8	=	28
x		+		−		x		
8	−	5	+	6	x	2	=	18
−		x		+		−		
2	+	6	x	8	−	5	=	59
=		=		=		=		
86		66		12		23		

142

							121
20	1	22	14	1	22	21	101
23	15	2	15	24	17	30	126
3	16	13	16	23	6	21	98
12	30	24	5	14	29	25	139
17	4	11	26	26	20	7	111
29	25	18	9	28	28	18	155
19	10	27	2	19	8	27	112
123	101	117	87	135	130	149	134

143

Circle = 9, Pentagon = 2, Square = 1, Star = 8.

144

Circle = 3, Pentagon = 9, Square = 2, Star = 6.

145

2	4	4	4	4	3
2	3	3	4	4	1
2	3	3	4	4	1
1	1	1	3	3	4
1	1	1	3	3	4
2	4	4	1	1	2

146

66 – Starting at the top and working clockwise, $12 + 3 = 15 \times 2 = 30 + 3 = 33 \times 2 = 66 + 3 = 69 \times 2 = 138$.

147

3	2	1	4
1	4	3	2
4	1	2	3
2	3	4	1

148

3	2	4	1
1	4	2	3
2	1	3	4
4	3	1	2

149

6	5	3	2	1	4
4	1	2	3	5	6
5	3	6	1	4	2
2	4	1	6	3	5
1	2	4	5	6	3
3	6	5	4	2	1

150

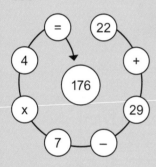

151

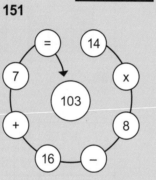

152

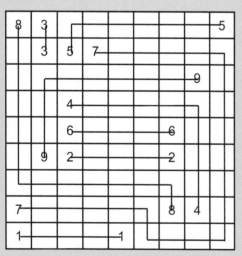

153

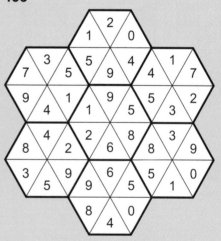

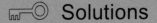

154

19 – 11 = 8, 8 x 4 = 32, 32 x 3 = 96, 96 – 18 = 78, 78 + 3 = 81, 81 ÷ 9 = 9, square root of 9 = 3

155

30 x 5 = 150, 150 ÷ 25 = 6, 6 x 9 = 54, 54 ÷ 2 = 27, 27 + 18 = 45, 45 x 2 = 90, 20% of 90 = 18

156

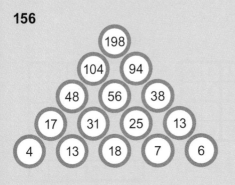

157

3	x	6	–	9	=	9
+		–		+		
2	+	5	x	7	=	49
x		x		x		
8	–	1	+	4	=	11
=		=		=		
40		1		64		

158

5	+	7	–	2	x	9	=	90
–		+		x		–		
2	x	5	+	9	–	7	=	12
x		x		–		+		
9	–	2	x	7	+	5	=	54
+		–		+		x		
7	+	9	x	5	–	2	=	78
=		=		=		=		
34		15		16		14		

159

							85
17	21	10	15	14	3	20	100
20	3	28	15	8	14	19	107
29	16	7	2	13	21	4	92
4	11	9	9	6	27	13	79
30	12	5	22	19	5	26	119
18	23	7	10	18	12	8	96
1	11	17	6	25	16	24	100
119	97	83	79	103	98	114	91

160

Circle = 3, Pentagon = 7, Square = 8, Star = 5.

161

Circle = 5, Pentagon = 4, Square = 6, Star = 2.

162

4	1	1	2	2	2
1	2	2	3	3	4
1	2	2	3	3	4
1	3	3	1	1	3
1	3	3	1	1	3
1	2	2	4	4	4

163

70 – Working clockwise from the top, 68 + 7 = 75 − 6 = 69 + 5 = 74 − 4 = 70 + 3 = 73 − 2 = 71.

164

3	2	4	1
4	1	3	2
2	4	1	3
1	3	2	4

165

1	4	3	2
3	2	1	4
4	1	2	3
2	3	4	1

166

2	1	3	4	5	6
6	4	5	2	1	3
3	6	2	5	4	1
4	5	1	6	3	2
1	2	4	3	6	5
5	3	6	1	2	4

167

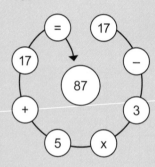

168

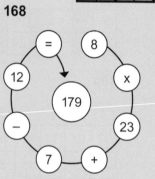

169

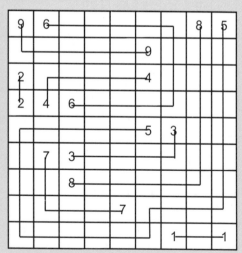

170

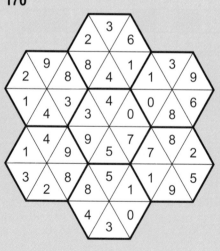

240

171

23 + 18 = 41, 41 x 3 = 123, 123 − 84 = 39, 39 ÷ 3 x 2 = 26, 26 ÷ 2 = 13, 13 + 19 = 32, 32 ÷ 4 x 3 = 24

172

7 x 9 = 63, 63 − 45 = 18, 18 + 6 = 24, 24 ÷ 4 = 6, 6 x 5 = 30, 30 x 3 = 90, 30% of 90 = 27

173

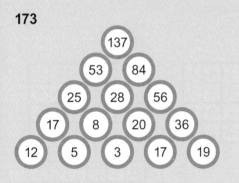

174

3	+	7	x	1	=	10
x		−		+		
6	−	5	x	9	=	9
+		x		x		
8	x	4	+	2	=	34
=		=		=		
26		8		20		

175

5	−	3	+	8	x	7	=	70
+		x		−		+		
8	+	7	−	5	x	3	=	30
x		−		x		−		
3	x	8	+	7	−	5	=	26
−		+		+		x		
7	−	5	x	3	+	8	=	14
=		=		=		=		
32		18		24		40		

176

							105
30	20	13	23	5	21	22	134
24	12	1	6	17	29	11	100
28	4	27	18	6	28	7	118
19	7	3	5	10	27	2	73
29	8	4	26	16	26	30	139
2	14	23	9	1	9	11	69
25	24	3	8	10	15	25	110
157	89	74	95	65	155	108	124

177

Circle = 7, Pentagon = 6, Square = 3, Star = 1.

178

Circle = 8, Pentagon = 1, Square = 7, Star = 4.

179

1	4	4	2	2	4
2	1	1	1	1	3
2	1	1	1	1	3
2	3	3	4	4	4
2	3	3	4	4	4
3	2	2	4	4	2

180

45 – Multiply the number in the outer point of the star by the adjacent number in the central hexagon to reach the number in the opposite point of the star.

181

3	4	2	1
2	1	3	4
4	3	1	2
1	2	4	3

182

2	1	4	3
3	4	1	2
4	2	3	1
1	3	2	4

183

1	5	3	4	2	6
2	6	4	3	1	5
3	2	6	5	4	1
4	1	5	6	3	2
6	4	1	2	5	3
5	3	2	1	6	4

184

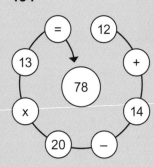

185

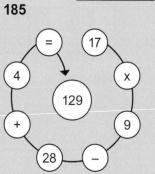

186

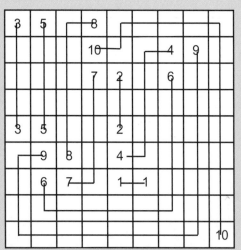

187

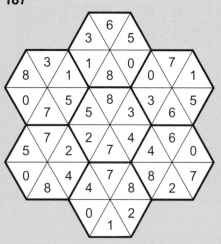

188

17 x 2 = 34, 34 + 28 = 62, 62 − 14 = 48, 48 ÷ 3 = 16, 16 x 5 = 80, 80 x 1.25 = 100, 14% of 100 = 14

189

165 ÷ 3 = 55, 55 + 11 = 66, 66 ÷ 6 = 11, 11² = 121, 121 − 16 = 105, 105 ÷ 21 = 5, 5 + 62 = 67

190

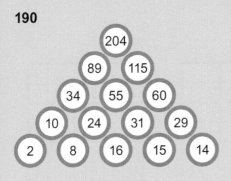

191

4	x	9	−	6	=	30
x		+		−		
3	+	7	x	1	=	10
+		−		+		
8	−	5	x	2	=	6
=		=		=		
20		11		7		

192

9	−	3	+	1	x	8	=	56
+		x		+		−		
1	x	9	−	8	+	3	=	4
x		−		x		+		
3	+	8	x	9	−	1	=	98
−		+		−		x		
8	−	1	+	3	x	9	=	90
=		=		=		=		
22		20		78		54		

193

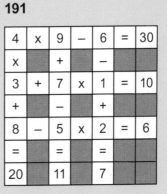

12	18	23	22	5	14	21	115
6	28	14	13	23	30	7	121
22	24	4	21	16	13	20	120
29	15	8	27	11	20	26	136
29	3	17	18	26	10	16	119
12	19	19	30	2	24	28	134
17	9	27	25	15	25	1	119

127	116	112	156	98	136	119	122

147

194

Circle = 4, Pentagon = 8, Square = 3, Star = 7.

195

Circle = 2, Pentagon = 5, Square = 8, Star = 3.

196

3	2	2	1	1	2
1	2	2	4	4	3
1	2	2	4	4	3
2	3	3	4	4	1
2	3	3	4	4	1
1	1	1	2	2	1

197

62 – Working clockwise from the top, 82 – 13 = 69 + 5 = 74 – 12 = 62.

198

4	1	3	2
3	2	4	1
2	4	1	3
1	3	2	4

199

2	1	4	3
4	3	2	1
1	4	3	2
3	2	1	4

200

5	4	1	6	3	2
2	3	6	1	4	5
4	5	3	2	6	1
1	6	2	4	5	3
3	2	4	5	1	6
6	1	5	3	2	4

201

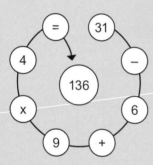

202

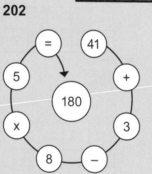

203

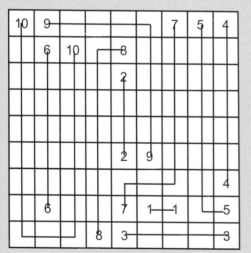

204

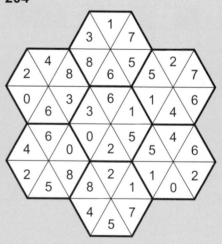

205

94 + 6 = 100, square root of 100 = 10, 10 + 25 = 35, 35 ÷ 7 = 5, 5^2 = 25, 25 x 7 = 175, 175 + 13 = 188

206

57 x 2 = 114, 114 ÷ 3 = 38, 38 + 11 = 49, square root of 49 = 7, 7 x 9 = 63, 63 − 8 = 55, 55 + 17 = 72

207

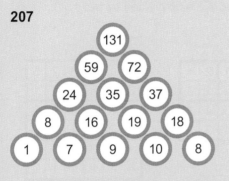

131
59 72
24 35 37
8 16 19 18
1 7 9 10 8

208

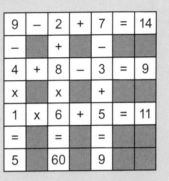

9	−	2	+	7	=	14
−		+		−		
4	+	8	−	3	=	9
x		x		+		
1	x	6	+	5	=	11
=		=		=		
5		60		9		

209

3	x	7	−	5	+	2	=	18
+		−		x		+		
5	−	2	x	7	+	3	=	24
x		x		−		x		
2	+	5	x	3	−	7	=	14
−		+		+		−		
7	+	3	x	2	−	5	=	15
=		=		=		=		
9		28		34		30		

210

							108
17	16	7	25	4	2	11	82
3	3	12	13	7	20	9	67
12	29	24	19	10	1	6	101
15	2	6	1	11	26	8	69
30	16	21	28	13	15	17	140
8	22	18	14	5	27	14	108
23	19	9	10	18	5	4	88
108	107	97	110	68	96	69	89

211

Circle = 4, Pentagon = 5, Square = 7, Star = 8.

212

Circle = 2, Pentagon = 7, Square = 4, Star = 9.

245

Solutions

213

4	4	4	1	1	2
2	3	3	3	3	1
2	3	3	3	3	1
4	2	2	1	1	4
4	2	2	1	1	4
1	3	3	1	1	3

214

28 – In opposite points of the star, the lower number is multiplied by the central number and the result is divided by two to equal the higher number, so 8 x 7 = 56 divided by two = 28.

215

1	2	4	3
4	3	1	2
3	4	2	1
2	1	3	4

216

3	1	2	4
4	2	1	3
2	3	4	1
1	4	3	2

217

3	1	4	6	2	5
2	6	5	3	4	1
4	3	1	2	5	6
5	2	6	1	3	4
1	5	3	4	6	2
6	4	2	5	1	3

218

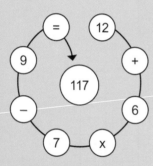

219

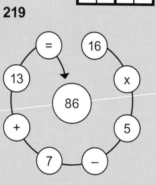

220

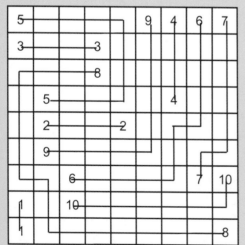

221

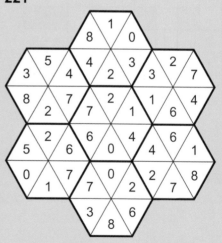

246

222

Square root of 9 = 3, 3 x 14 = 42, 42 + 6 = 48, 48 ÷ 4 = 12, 12² = 144, 144 ÷ 9 = 16, 16 x 3 = 48

223

329 – 4 = 325, 325 ÷ 5 = 65, 65 x 2 = 130, 130 + 10 = 140, 140 ÷ 20 = 7, 7 – 3 = 4, square root of 4 = 2

224

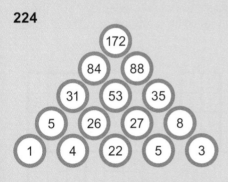

225

4	x	3	–	7	=	5
+		x		+		
1	x	6	+	9	=	15
x		+		–		
8	–	5	x	2	=	6
=		=		=		
40		23		14		

226

9	–	3	+	4	x	7	=	70
x		+		+		–		
4	+	7	x	9	–	3	=	96
–		x		–		x		
7	x	9	–	3	+	4	=	64
+		–		x		+		
3	+	4	x	7	–	9	=	40
=		=		=		=		
32		86		70		25		

227

							123
21	27	30	1	4	6	19	108
20	9	16	25	22	5	7	104
2	26	8	15	5	26	8	90
10	2	23	22	17	1	28	103
28	6	27	13	21	24	18	137
3	25	14	3	7	11	29	92
20	4	29	30	12	24	23	142
104	99	147	109	88	97	132	115

228

Circle = 7, Pentagon = 8, Square = 4, Star = 2.

229

Circle = 4, Pentagon = 6, Square = 2, Star = 8.

Solutions

230

1	1	1	4	4	3
3	4	4	1	1	3
3	4	4	1	1	3
2	4	4	2	2	2
2	4	4	2	2	2
4	3	3	1	1	2

231

186 – Working clockwise from the top, multiply the first number by two, then deduct three, then multiply by four, then deduct five, then multiply by six (the question mark is replaced by 186), then deduct seven to reach the number in the middle.

232

2	4	1	3
3	1	2	4
4	2	3	1
1	3	4	2

233

1	3	2	4
2	4	1	3
4	2	3	1
3	1	4	2

234

5	2	4	3	6	1
1	3	6	2	4	5
3	4	5	1	2	6
6	1	2	4	5	3
4	6	3	5	1	2
2	5	1	6	3	4

235

236

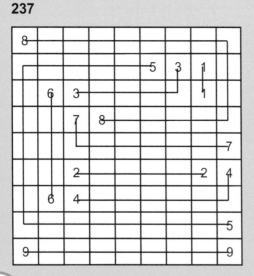

237

238

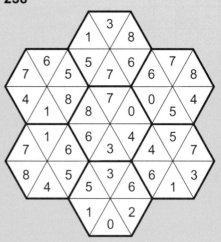

248

239

87 ÷ 3 = 29, 29 + 7 = 36, square root of 36 = 6, 6 x 9 = 54, 54 − 16 = 38, 38 ÷ 2 = 19, 19 + 15 = 34

240

84 ÷ 7 = 12, 12² = 144, 144 ÷ 9 = 16, square root of 16 = 4, 4 x 13 = 52, 52 ÷ 2 = 26, 26 + 45 = 71

241

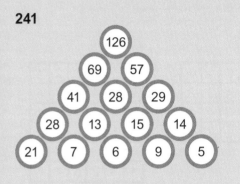

126
69 57
41 28 29
28 13 15 14
21 7 6 9 5

242

2	x	5	−	9	=	1
+		x		−		
7	x	1	+	3	=	10
−		+		x		
6	+	4	x	8	=	80
=		=		=		
3		9		48		

243

4	+	3	x	9	−	6	=	57
x		+		−		+		
6	−	4	+	3	x	9	=	45
−		x		+		x		
9	−	6	x	4	+	3	=	15
+		−		x		−		
3	x	9	−	6	+	4	=	25
=		=		=		=		
18		33		60		41		

244

							107
9	27	21	19	12	26	19	133
12	18	26	5	10	20	25	116
2	13	17	27	1	16	13	89
25	4	24	10	23	24	15	125
14	20	18	14	9	6	23	104
22	28	3	7	17	22	8	107
11	21	11	29	16	30	15	133
95	131	120	111	88	144	118	100

245

Circle = 9, Pentagon = 8, Square = 4, Star = 5.

246

Circle = 4, Pentagon = 8, Square = 2, Star = 6.

Solutions 🔑

247

3	2	2	3	3	3
4	4	4	1	1	2
4	4	4	1	1	2
3	1	1	1	1	2
3	1	1	1	1	2
2	2	2	4	4	3

248

81 – Divide the number in the outer point of the star by the adjacent number in the central hexagon, then square this total to reach the number in the opposite point of the star.

249

3	4	1	2
2	1	4	3
4	2	3	1
1	3	2	4

250

3	2	1	4
1	4	3	2
2	3	4	1
4	1	2	3

251

5	1	3	6	2	4
2	6	4	1	3	5
3	2	6	4	5	1
4	5	1	3	6	2
6	4	5	2	1	3
1	3	2	5	4	6

252

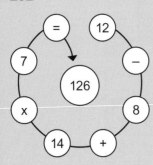

253

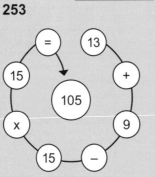

254

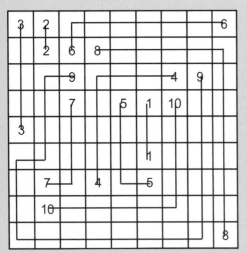

255

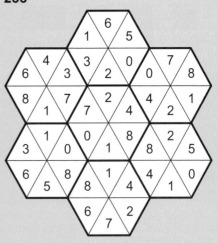

256

76 − 4 = 72, 72 ÷ 8 = 9, 9² = 81, 81 + 39 = 120, 120 ÷ 3 = 40, 40 − 4 = 36, 36 ÷ 4 = 9

257

36 ÷ 3 = 12, 12 − 4 = 8, 8² = 64, 64 x 2 = 128, 128 ÷ 4 = 32, 32 ÷ 2 = 16, 16 − 11 = 5

258

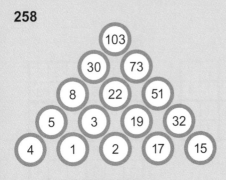

259

9	−	1	+	4	=	12
−		+		x		
3	+	7	x	5	=	50
+		x		−		
2	x	6	+	8	=	20
=		=		=		
8		48		12		

260

7	+	3	x	8	−	2	=	78
−		x		+		+		
2	x	8	−	7	+	3	=	12
x		−		x		x		
3	+	7	−	2	x	8	=	64
+		+		−		−		
8	−	2	x	3	+	7	=	25
=		=		=		=		
23		19		27		33		

261

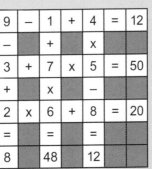

							143
28	3	13	27	1	10	14	96
5	14	23	12	22	28	11	115
24	3	2	6	17	8	21	81
7	4	5	13	29	2	6	66
18	8	29	25	11	12	7	110
16	26	15	30	4	10	20	121
16	30	1	9	15	19	9	99
114	88	88	122	99	89	88	87

262

Circle = 6, Pentagon = 2, Square = 1, Star = 8.

263

Circle = 1, Pentagon = 7, Square = 5, Star = 6.

264

2	3	3	2	2	3
1	1	1	2	2	1
1	1	1	2	2	1
2	4	4	3	3	3
2	4	4	3	3	3
1	4	4	1	1	4

265

512 – The numbers in the outer points of the star are the cubes of the adjacent numbers in the central hexagon.

266

3	1	4	2
4	2	1	3
1	3	2	4
2	4	3	1

267

1	4	2	3
3	2	1	4
2	3	4	1
4	1	3	2

268

3	1	4	6	2	5
2	6	5	1	4	3
1	5	2	4	3	6
6	4	3	5	1	2
4	3	6	2	5	1
5	2	1	3	6	4

269

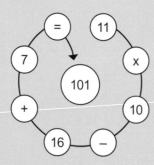

270

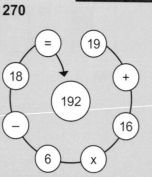

271

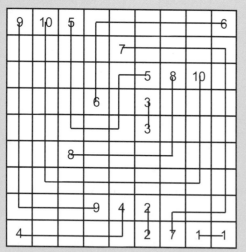

272

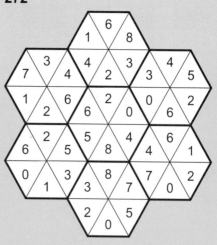

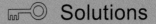

273

$13^2 = 169$, $169 + 31 = 200$, $200 \div 4 = 50$, $50 \times 5 = 250$, $250 + 25 = 275$, $275 - 125 = 150$, $150 \div 3 = 50$

274

$59 - 26 = 33$, $33 \div 11 = 3$, $3 \times 7 = 21$, $21 + 14 = 35$, $35 + 7 = 42$, $42 \div 6 = 7$, $7 \times 4 = 28$

275

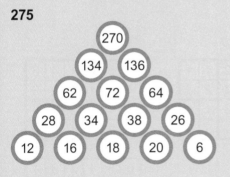

276

4	–	2	x	8	=	16
+		x		–		
7	+	5	x	1	=	12
–		+		x		
3	x	9	–	6	=	21
=		=		=		
8		19		42		

277

4	+	6	–	1	x	9	=	81
–		x		+		–		
1	x	9	+	6	–	4	=	11
x		+		x		+		
6	–	4	x	9	+	1	=	19
+		–		–		x		
9	+	1	x	4	–	6	=	34
=		=		=		=		
27		57		59		36		

278

								87
30	5	4	5	18	28	30	120
21	21	23	29	15	4	24	137
27	6	17	26	3	22	9	110
2	26	20	3	24	10	16	101
14	25	25	19	11	17	1	112
29	2	12	19	30	8	23	123
20	13	1	18	28	27	7	114
143	98	102	119	129	116	110	97

279

Circle = 6, Cross = 2, Pentagon = 3, Square = 8, Star = 7.

280

Circle = 1, Cross = 3, Pentagon = 8, Square = 6, Star = 5.

281

4	2	2	1	1	4
1	3	3	2	2	1
1	3	3	2	2	1
3	4	4	2	2	4
3	4	4	2	2	4
3	1	1	1	1	4

282

58 – Each single-digit number is squared and the result is added to the central number to give the number in the opposite point of the star.

283

2	4	1	3
3	1	2	4
4	2	3	1
1	3	4	2

284

3	2	4	1
1	4	2	3
2	3	1	4
4	1	3	2

285

5	3	2	1	4	6
4	6	1	5	2	3
2	4	6	3	1	5
3	1	5	4	6	2
1	2	3	6	5	4
6	5	4	2	3	1

286

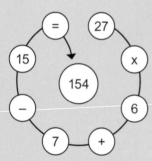

287

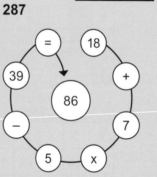

288

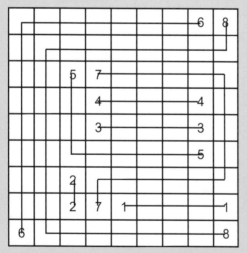

289

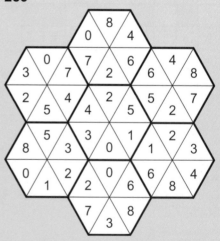

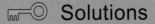

290

75 x 7 = 525, 525 ÷ 25 = 21, 21 ÷ 7 = 3, 3 x 16 = 48, 48 ÷ 6 = 8, 8 ÷ 4 = 2, 2 x 98 = 196

291

87 + 9 = 96, 96 ÷ 12 = 8, 8 + 12 = 20, 20 + 1 = 21, 21 ÷ 7 = 3, 3 x 19 = 57, 57 + 73 = 130

292

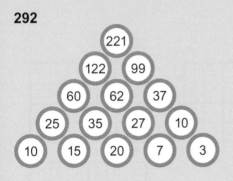

293

1	x	7	+	4	=	11
+		+		x		
5	x	9	–	3	=	42
–		x		+		
2	+	6	x	8	=	64
=		=		=		
4		96		20		

294

3	+	8	–	7	x	5	=	20
x		–		x		+		
5	x	7	+	8	–	3	=	40
+		x				x		
7	+	3	x	5	–	8	=	42
–		+		+		–		
8	–	5	x	3	+	7	=	16
=		=		=		=		
14		8		54		57		

295

							75
6	27	13	5	18	19	7	95
28	23	12	17	24	8	9	121
20	12	4	26	14	6	19	101
11	16	23	17	13	8	16	104
24	3	9	20	7	25	21	109
22	10	29	15	18	22	14	130
10	21	11	2	15	30	1	90
121	112	101	102	109	118	87	80

296

Circle = 1, Cross = 5, Pentagon = 4, Square = 9, Star = 7.

297

Circle = 3, Cross = 2, Pentagon = 9, Square = 6, Star = 7.

Solutions 🔑

298

1	4	4	1	1	1
3	1	1	4	4	4
3	1	1	4	4	4
2	3	3	3	3	2
2	3	3	3	3	2
1	4	4	2	2	4

299

147 – Each two-digit number is multiplied by 10 and the central number is deducted from this sum to give the number in the opposite point of the star.

300

3	1	4	2
2	4	1	3
4	2	3	1
1	3	2	4

301

3	2	4	1
4	1	3	2
2	3	1	4
1	4	2	3

302

5	4	6	3	1	2
3	2	1	5	4	6
6	5	4	2	3	1
2	1	3	6	5	4
4	6	5	1	2	3
1	3	2	4	6	5

303

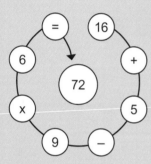

304

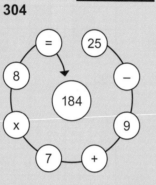

305

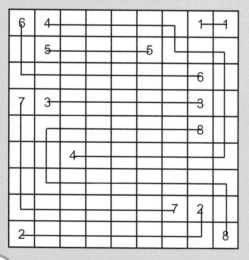